Saving Children

Saving Children

Diary of a Buchenwald Survivor and Rescuer

Jack Werber

With William B. Helmreich

TRANSACTION PUBLISHERS

New Brunswick (U.S.A.) and London (U.K.)

Library of Congress Catalog Number: 95-23909
ISBN: 1-56000-250-6
Printed in the United States of America

Library of Congress Cataloging-in-Publication Data

Werber, Jack.
   Saving children : diary of a Buchenwald survivor and rescuer / Jack Werber with William B. Helmreich.
      p. cm.
   ISBN 1-56000-250-6 (alk. paper)
   1. Jews—Poland—Radom (Radom)—Biography.   2. Holocaust, Jewish (1939–1945)—Poland—Radom (Radom)—Personal narratives.   3. Werber, Jack.   4. Buchenwald (Germany : Concentration camp)   5. Radom (Radom, Poland)—Biography.   I. Helmreich, William B.   II. Title.
DS135.P63W416   1995
943.8′4—dc20
                                                      95-23909
                                                         CIP

For my Children

Martin and Bracha	David and Ellie
and their children,	and their children,
Chava, Benjamin, and Talia	Shoshana, Tovah, and Joshua

and to all their future generations

Master of the Universe, send us our Messiah, for we have no more strength to suffer. Show me a sign, O God. Otherwise...otherwise...I rebel against Thee. If Thou dost not keep The Covenant, Then neither will I keep that Promise, and it is all over, we are through being Thy chosen people, Thy peculiar treasure.

—The Rebbe of Kotzk,
  from Chaim Potok's *The Promise*

Contents

Introduction

"From Weimar, through forests, on soggy, marshy ground, a ten-kilometer road winds its way toward Buchenwald. Paved with asphalt, mixed in with the sweat and blood of thousands of victims who there breathed the last gasp from their tormented souls. Off to the side, snow can still be seen, but on the road itself, it has disappeared, trampled into oblivion by the steps of those who trod on it. A heavy curtain of fog has descended on the marchers, as if to conceal from the world the shame of what is happening here.

No other human being can be seen for miles. From time to time, one can spy, through the mist, an SS automobile on the shiny road. From the distance, the silhouettes of the marchers become clearer, part of a larger mass of thousands of bareheaded people, many carrying rucksacks and even suitcases on their backs. Eyes bulging with shock and fear, their hands behind their necks, their hair disheveled, they run along the road past cars and trucks filled with modern weaponry—with the sights of rifles trained on them. The wild dogs strain at their leashes, as vicious as their owners, pouncing sometimes upon one person, sometimes upon another, tearing the flesh from those whom they chase.

One man bends down to tie his shoelace, is shot, and falls with the uncompleted words of the *Shema* prayer on his lips. A heavy-set man, in desperate straits, begs the guard for a drop of water. Mocking him, the guard says: 'Fool, slurp up your own blood,' and gives his answer with his gun. The unfortunate victim drops to the ground like a felled log, the words of Jesus Christ on his lips. The third falls, the tenth, the hundredth, all lie drowning in their blood as it collects on the road's hard surface.

As they run, sweat pours forth from their exhausted bodies, despite the bitter winter cold. They throw off their coats, discard their luggage, and even remove their shoes from their swollen feet. In this manner, they come to a fork in the road. One sign points to the concentration camp, the other to the living quarters of the SS. Beneath the first sign is a drunk with a red nose, a priest with a bible in his hand, a political with a red bow tie, and a Jew with a hooked nose. The second sign depicts four others, all of them German officers, rifles at the ready.

At the edge of the forest is a sign with a skull and crossbones: 'Danger! All Trespassers Will be Shot Without Warning!' A few hundred meters ahead is a large boulder with an eagle and a swastika engraved upon it. To the left and right of the rock are two gates, each guarded by SS men. Next to the right-hand gate is the main guardhouse and on the left is the post office. The gates swing open and we are greeted by wild screams and the thud of rifle butts hard against our bodies. We are driven from the camp entrance to the barracks. Several meters from the post office we see engraved, on a wooden signpost, a drawing of three men in zebra-like uniforms, running quickly down what looks like a speedway, singing as they do so.

Our bodies are covered with black-and-blue marks, our breathing is labored, and our clothes are torn by the dogs, drenched in our own blood. This is how we arrive at Buchenwald—in a state of total and utter exhaustion. On each side of the gate is a turret, both attached to a building on the side. The entrance itself is under a three-story building in the center, which contains a balcony above the second floor, along which are machine guns trained on the camp grounds, a watchtower with a clock above the top of the structure, and searchlights, which light up the entire camp at night.

To the left is a bunker for the prisoners; it is a punishment area for those who have committed 'crimes' against the Germans. To the right are administrative offices. Outside are high steel gates with letters made of wrought iron which proclaim 'To each his own.' Above that is written 'Right or Wrong, my Fatherland.'

Immediately outside the camp is the home of the Camp Commandant. Next to it are two cannons of World War I vintage.

Across from the Commandant's house is a zoo, on whose wall are written instructions pertaining to the proper care and feeding of animals. Aware that a new transport with 'fresh material' has arrived, the rulers come running, as if to a giant celebration. *Standartenführer* (Commandant) Karl Koch and *Lagerführer* Schubert, and Sergeants Ullman and Abraham, have been waiting impatiently for us and we are now ordered to form rows of four to the accompaniment of much laughter and jokes by the soldiers about our appearance. We are counted and chased into the camp, where we begin our new lives."

* * *

After my liberation from Buchenwald, I wrote down these recollections of my arrival there five and half years earlier. My life in Buchenwald was an eternity. It affected every part of me, and remains with me at all times. It shaped the man I became, and influenced everything I have done since.

Over the years I wrote notes about my life in Buchenwald, without any specific purpose in mind. I never planned to write a book. I even wondered if perhaps too many personal accounts of the Holocaust had already been published. It is Millie, my beloved wife of nearly fifty years, who insisted that my account of the Buchenwald nightmare needed to be told. The rise of revisionism requires that all of the survivors who can, should preserve their stories. Each survivor had a different experience. By presenting a chorus of different voices we disprove the theories of the Holocaust deniers. We owe this to our parents and other loved ones, friends and martyrs who did not survive the war. We also owe it to our children and future generations of mankind. I am indebted to Millie for, among other things, urging me to complete this task, for her insights, and inspiration and for painstakingly reviewing the work in progress. Her love and devotion knows no end. I also want to give special thanks to my son, Martin, whose suggestions and editorial changes, greatly improved this work.

1

Growing Up in Radom

We were eight children and I was the youngest. I was born in Radom, Poland, a city well known for its tanneries and shoe factories. Nearly a third of Radom's prewar population of 100,000 was Jewish. Most of the Jews in my home-town were killed along with 90 percent of Poland's Jews during World War II. With one exception, my father and all of my brothers and sisters shared the same fate. Mannes, my oldest brother, had immigrated to America before World War I, actually before I was born. Other than Mannes, I am the only survivor.

I don't remember my mother very well since she died when I was only six. All I can recall is that she loved us but was sick most of the time. She died in Warsaw where she was seeking medical attention. At the time, my sisters Rivka and Dorka and I were away in the country at a bungalow we had rented for the summer. A neighbor came to tell my sisters that my mother had died. Our family decided to bury her the next day in Radom, about sixty miles away. It was, however, against the law to transport a body to another locality for burial. So my mother's body was dressed and propped up in a wagon as if she were alive. The wagon was stopped en route and the authorities discovered what we were doing. We had no choice but to bury my mother right there in the town of Karchew, near Otwock.

By today's standards it might seem that our apartment was small and cramped, but for those times it was considered quite luxurious—three rooms, a living room, a bedroom, and a kitchen, for

5

nine of us, including the maid. I slept in the same room as my sisters until they were married and the maid slept in the kitchen.

We were relatively well off, but life was far from easy for most people in those days. Large families, with six or seven children, often lived in one room. Indoor plumbing was extremely rare. As a rule there was no sink, just one pan for clean water and another for dirty water. Communal outhouses served all the residents of apartment buildings.

By comparison, our apartment was the Taj Mahal. It even had an individual toilet, the size of a telephone booth, that was partitioned off from the kitchen. We also had a sink with running water, but if you wanted to take a bath it was necessary to go to the public city baths, five minutes away. In all of Radom, with a population of maybe 100,000 people, there were, perhaps, ten apartment buildings with bathtubs.

Despite these conditions life there was very pleasant. There was a spirit of togetherness among families. The common view of the life of prewar Polish Jewry is rather grim. One pictures intense poverty and pious old Jews studying Torah. In fact, this was a very exciting time in Jewish history. There were cultural and communal organizations of all types, which enriched the community economically and spiritually. Ezra gave aid to the needy, Hachnassat Orchim provided for newcomers in town, and Bikkur Cholim visited the sick. There were orphanages, old age homes, Hachnassat Kallah (New Brides Fund), a fresh-air fund, sports clubs, yeshivas, and Jewish schools. Together, they contributed enormously towards making Radom an intimate and caring community. Who knows what the Jewish community would have looked like after another generation had it been allowed to continue to flourish?

While there were large numbers of traditional Jews, many others were exploring different avenues of Jewish expression. It was a vigorous, open marketplace of competing Jewish ideologies. There were the religious, Jewish culturalists, and the secularists. There were the socialists and capitalists, Zionists and anti-Zionists. And there were multiple combinations of all of the above.

My father did not remarry until several years after my mother's death. By then my sisters were already married and had moved out of our house. He was about sixty years old at the time. On the day of the wedding I wasn't sure what was happening, but I knew something was going on. I saw my father putting on his holiday clothes and so I went over to consult with my sister Rivka, who lived a few blocks away. She confirmed my suspicion that father was getting married that night and suggested that I go home and go to sleep as if nothing was going on. I went back to the house, but, of course, I couldn't sleep. I was too excited and I lay awake in bed wondering what effect a new woman in the household would have on my life. I finally fell asleep just after I heard my father and his new wife come through the door.

The next morning, when I woke up, my father simply said to me, "Go say good morning and kiss your 'aunt.'" That's how our new relationship began. In those days a stepmother was often referred to as an aunt. I was reluctant to do so right away, but I didn't want to be disrespectful of my father's wishes. So I went into the other room, and instead of saying good morning, I busied myself for a moment with the flowerpot on the window sill before leaving the house for school. She turned out to be a very nice woman and was always good to me. Children generally had strong feelings about a stepmother replacing a mother, but because of her attitude towards me, we never had a problem. I often asked her advice, in part, because I wanted to show her that I valued her opinion. Having no children of her own, it wasn't long before she came to see me as her own child.

My father started out as a furrier. He would go to wealthy peoples' homes and make coats or jackets for them. He needed to supplement his income by working as a capmaker. In addition, he rented orchards for the summer, picked the fruit, and then sold it to retailers. In short, it took three trades for him to eke out a living for his family.

Through sheer determination and perseverance, he eventually managed to open up his own shop and devote himself exclusively to the fur trade. He had people working for him and by the time I was born our family was comfortably middle class. In fact, we owned the building that I was born in and grew up in, Zeromskiego, Number 14. The narrow front of the three floor walk-up building had a handsome Renaissance exterior. It blended in well on Zeromskiego Street, the main street in Radom, which was lined with many elegant shops. The building had twenty-nine apartments above and behind my father's store, which was located at the front of the ground floor. There was a long narrow courtyard stretching all the way back to the end of the building. At the far end of the courtyard was the headquarters of Hashomer Hatzair, a Zionist youth movement I belonged to. Our store was identified by the beautiful stuffed leopard in the window, surrounded by expensive furs—collars, coats, and jackets. The sign over the door simply stated my father's name, Josef Maier Werber.

Even though we had a reasonably profitable business, we still had our problems. There was always the fear of robberies which occurred from time to time. On one such occasion, in 1937, we were robbed by thieves from Warsaw. During the day they had gained access to the basement under the apartments via an unlocked door in the courtyard. They broke through a partition in the basement and dug a small tunnel to reach underneath the fur storeroom at the rear of our store.

The thieves knew exactly where to end the tunnel because they sent an elegantly dressed woman into the store on the pretext of wanting to buy a fox stole. My brother Moishe had gone into the storeroom and she had followed him. While there, she stamped on the floor with her shoes several times, claiming that she was cold. It sounded plausible since it was January but, in reality, she was signaling the thieves, who were waiting below, where to end the tunnel.

As usual, the gate to the courtyard was locked at 11:00 P.M. by the night watchman, who patrolled the grounds with his dog. In order to gain admittance after that hour, tenants and visitors had to ring a bell to alert the night watchman. He would then let in those who belonged there through the courtyard gate.

Around 1:00 A.M., a well-dressed man, who was one of the thieves, rang the bell. He told the watchman that he was waiting to meet someone in front of the Rzymsky Hotel which was across the street and that the man had not yet shown up. "Here's five *zlotys*. Please wait for him and when you see him tell him to go inside the hotel and wait for me in the lobby." In this way, he succeeded in getting the watchman to leave the courtyard, thus allowing the thieves to get inside and reach the tunnel they had dug under our store.

As a result, the thieves were able to steal a large number of furs and because the next day, January 3rd, was a Catholic holiday, the theft was not discovered until later. How did we learn of it? A tenant, going through his own storage bin, found some furs in the basement that the thieves, in their haste to get away, had dropped and left on the ground. When we found out, we demanded that the watchman explain how this could have happened. He became very nervous and said that he was gone, at the most, for half an hour because a man had called him away. Then, without our knowledge, in an attempt to make up for what had happened, he informed the police. There was an investigation and a few months later, the thieves were caught and sent to jail.

By going to the police, the watchman had only made matters worse. He didn't know how these thieves operated. After a burglary, we, like other such victims, would go to a certain tavern in town notorious for its underworld clientele. We would wait until we were approached by one of the regulars who asked us what kind of merchandise we were seeking. We were immediately recognizable because average citizens only went there in situations like this. We then told him what was missing and he would invariably tell us to come back the following day. When we did, we would have a "discussion" with the thieves' "representatives" and negotiate a price in exchange for the return of the merchandise. I might mention that when we did get it back, nothing, not even a needle, was ever missing. After all, these were "honorable" thieves who lived up to their code of conduct. Going to the police was a "breach of faith," and the thieves could no longer negotiate with us. Since the thieves were sent to jail, we never got any of the furs back. As fate would have it, I crossed paths with the thieves once again. I was thrown into the same cell as them when I was first jailed by the Nazis. I never told them who I was, but I did gain their confidence. I listened to them with amusement as they bragged about what a great job they had done breaking into our store.

At the age of five, I was sent to *cheder* where I received a Jewish education. We studied *Chumash* (Bible), Talmud, Hebrew language, and a little Polish. The *cheder* had four rooms, which made it a pretty big *cheder*. The *rebbe* and his family slept in one of them. The day was long, maybe ten hours, but we found ways to have some fun, particularly since the *rebbe* was an easy target of our pranks. For example, he occasionally fell asleep during class, his head resting on the table. We would take a red stick of sealant, melt it with a candle, and paste his beard to the table. We then tapped on the table to wake him up, and when he did, he found that he was unable to lift his beard. Another prank exploited the *rebbe's* deathly fear of mice. We would roll a gray ball near him and he, thinking it was a mouse, would panic and usually end up jumping on the table.

Nevertheless, I took my studies pretty seriously. I had to because my father was very concerned about my progress. Every *Shabbes*, after a delicious steaming bowl of *chulent* stew, I had to report to my father about what I had learned during the week.

Most children became apprentices by the time they were twelve years old, sometimes even younger. But my father wanted me to continue studying, since he could at last afford to keep one of his children in school. And so I was enrolled in a well-known Jewish high school, *Chovevei Da'at*, or *Przyjaciol Wiedzy*, as it was called in Polish. There I studied Hebrew, Polish, history, algebra, and other subjects. In general, only those with money could attend. There were no scholarships in those days. As a result, there were many brilliant kids who couldn't go because they couldn't afford it.

We were called "the Golden Youths," in part because high school in Poland was very important; it was the equivalent of college. We didn't wear yarmulkes there because it was a cultural, as opposed to, religious school. There were eight classes in high school. I wanted to be a lawyer but because of the *numerus clausus* there was almost no chance of achieving that goal. School ended at 5:00, and afterwards I did my homework and then went to help out in the workshop. In general, I had very little contact with Polish Christian youths because it was a very anti-Semitic society. Certainly, I had no Polish friends. We were basically second-class citizens. If a Jewish boy walked on the same side of the street as a Christian boy and he was identified as a Jew, there was a pretty good chance he'd get beaten up or at least smacked.

Our summers were spent in a cottage in the country, in either Garbatka or Antoniowka, both small villages not too far from Radom. Usually a peasant would move out of his house into the barn for the summer and would rent his house for the season. There was no formal entertainment and our days basically consisted of sitting out near the woods, taking walks, reading, and just relaxing.

As a child I didn't find this very interesting and I far preferred to go on trips with my Uncle Zysel. He was a tailor, and he would take me along when he sold his goods in the markets of the neighboring towns. I would watch with fascination as Uncle Zysel used various sales techniques to entice the peasants into purchasing his wares. Even though he was a man in his seventies, he would appeal for sympathy by proclaiming "Buy from an orphan!" The markets had a carnival-like atmosphere. There were all sorts of games, using numbers, that were played. A favorite of mine was an organ grinder with a bird that, for a few *groschen,* would pick out with his beak an envelope and if you were lucky there would be a small present in it.

For recreation, the nonreligious were avid theater and film fans. My family also frequently saw films in the local theaters. Before talking films became widely available movies were without sound. A band sat in the front, under the stage—their heads were visible from our seats—and played accompanying music. There was a light near the band to enable them to read their notes. The choice of music depended upon what was happening on the screen. So, for example, when the horses would ride across the screen, they played faster. They showed mostly American movies—featuring Buster Keaton, Charlie Chaplin, Jean Harlow, and later, Clark Gable. The first talking movie I saw, I believe, was, *Under the Roofs of Paris.*

There were four movie houses in Radom, plus one theater. The films changed every week. It cost only pennies to attend, and so they were always crowded. I went maybe twice a week to see all of the new pictures, usually on Saturday night or on Sunday. As a rule, religious Jews didn't go to the movies. Shows started at 12:00 noon and refreshments were sold in the theater lobby. The seats were made of wood, and weren't upholstered. There were three sections, with third class, the cheapest, all the way up front. Such entertainment may seem like small pleasures when looked at today, but at the time they were exciting and deeply satisfying, for it was all that we had.

Since my mother had died when I was very young, everyone pampered and spoiled me. When I was eight or nine years old my brother Daniel bought a camera for me. This was something really special since no one my age had a camera. My father tried to compensate for my loss and was protective like a mother. He wasn't strict with me at all. I was a good boy in general. I never heard a loud word from my father, nor from any of my sisters and brothers. They used to take me everywhere with them. For example, they took me along whenever they went to the movies or the theater. I also learned to play the violin. My older brothers never had lessons but I was the youngest and my father could afford it by then.

My father was strictly Orthodox but not a hasid. After my mother died my father established a *shtibl* (small synagogue) in our apartment where we *davened* every Shabbes morning and afterwards my father gave a *kiddush*. It was basically a furriers' and capmakers' minyan. Like my father earlier in his career, many furriers had to be capmakers as well in order to make a living.

After school, about ten or so kids played in the courtyard with a ball made of rags. We also had a game similar to billiards that involved hitting one hazelnut with another. I remember those times with great fondness. As I became older, childhood recreation made way for my serious involvement with Hashomer Hatzair. We were going to change the world and had little time for child's play. In Hashomer Hatzair we believed that there was no future for Jewry in Europe. Jews had to rebuild their ancient land in Palestine, and in the process rebuild themselves as new Jews. The reclamation of the land and physical labor were critical to this process. The society we would build would be a socialist one, with true justice for all. The immediate goal was to settle in Palestine in kibbutzim. Hashomer Hatzair gave us a vision and a community of friends who shared common convictions and were committed to each other's well being. It gave us a feeling of brotherhood which cannot be easily replaced.

In reflecting on those years, I recall fondly a wide cast of characters who resided in our house and who are no more. Meyer, the carpenter, was a busybody with big ears who had to know everything that was going on. A well-known local rabbi, who lived in the building, had a mentally ill daughter who constantly called him names. The tenants would try to goad her into talking more about her father so that she could put on a show. Then there was a tailor, Mottl, who had a gramophone. And one was an old jewelry repairman named Velvel. He lived in one room. The only sound we ever heard coming from the room was his clock going "tick-tock, tick-tock." He fought constantly with the tailor over the loud music that came from the gramophone.

Velvel, the jeweler, had a daughter, Polcia. She had a picture in their apartment of Zysha Breitbart, a famous Jewish strongman. He could wrestle, bend iron bars, and break through chains with his teeth. She fell in love with him even though, to my knowledge, she never got to meet him personally. She would carry on monologues for hours with the large photograph of him that hung on the wall. Mostly she talked about how she loved him and how she was going to marry him. She was no longer a teenager, she was an adult. It's not that she believed he could actually hear her. It's just that she was infatuated with him and liked the idea of talking to him privately.

Zysha Breitbart himself was a household name among the Jews of Poland. He appeared on the stage and in circuses. He was an incredibly powerful man. He once lay down under a plank, allowed a truck to drive over it, and amazingly, he survived! His end, however, was very sad. He was competing in tests of strength against a Gentile in a circus in Radom. For one part of the competition, Zysha tried to put a large nail through a large wooden plank with his bare hand. He hit it so hard that the nail went completely through the plank and accidentally entered his knee. It became infected and he died from the wound. There was no penicillin in those days to treat infections.

Directly underneath us was Hersch Nachman and his family. He lived with his wife and six children in three rooms, and on top of that they took in boarders. His wife cooked for her guests as well. Two actors boarded with Hersch Nachman for a while. One night the actors climbed out through a window to avoid paying the rent, and quickly left town. Unfortunately, Hersch Nachman had many other boarders besides these actors, who didn't pay. Whenever this happened we would hear shouts of "*Ganovim!*" or "*Skandal!*" coming from the apartment.

Even though life was very difficult and people had to struggle hard to make a living, they never lost their sense of humor, their ability to laugh at life. Take, for example, Pesach Milman who had a small shoe store inside the courtyard. Every day we'd yell down: "Pesach, when is *Shavuous*?"

I'll never forget Henoch, the son of Sosre the grocer, a real *shlimazel*. Whatever he tried to do he failed. He was not too bright and people enjoyed making fun of him. At one point he peddled socks from shop to shop. So, as a practical joke, the boys tried on the socks over their muddy shoes. My father, however, had pity on him and whenever he caught the boys bothering Henoch, he made them stop.

The apartment houses in Radom were built around courtyards, creating a real sense of community. The whole building was like one large extended family. A neighbor would come in for a cup of sugar or for a few eggs. Mottl, the tailor, would play songs by putting his gramophone in the window so that we could all listen to them. People would yell out: "Mottl, put on Rosenblatt, or some other *chazzan*, or a Yiddish folk singer like Ben-Zion Witler or Sidor Belarsky." He was a friendly fellow and usually accommodated these requests. In our workshop on the floor above our apartment, twelve furriers sang and joked as they stretched, cut, and seamed skins together.

There was another shop in our building in which seamstresses worked and when they heard the furriers singing, they would join in too. And if Mottl the tailor heard the people singing he would try to drown it out with the music from the gramophone. To me it sometimes sounded like a musical Tower of Babel.

On Friday afternoon and Saturday, all the Jews closed their stores for *Shabbes*, with the exception of Kurover, the pharmacist, who wasn't observant. But even Kurover was closed on Yom Kippur. Friday evening, we went to the smaller *beis medrash* (house of study) where Israel Cooper was the *ba'al t'filah* (cantor). He had a most beautiful voice. Gershon Yoffe was the *chazzan* in the larger synagogue. He sang like an opera singer, but I found the *ba'al t'filah* in the *beis medrash* more pleasant to listen to. His voice was sweeter and he sang from the heart. My father also preferred the *beis medrash*, which, generally speaking, was for the common folk, to the larger synagogue. Actually, we had reserved seats in both places, which you bought and kept for life. One thing both houses of worship had in common was a choir. In 1937 Gershon Yoffe retired and we engaged a talented young cantor from Vilna named Moishe Rontal.

In fact, I was *bar-mitzvahed* in the *beis medrash*. Nothing fancy. It took place during the week, on a Thursday. I was called to the Torah and then we had a little vodka and some herring with egg kichel. Everybody made a *l'chaim*, and that was it. My father, my brothers and sisters, and other close family members, were there. You didn't send out invitations in those days. However, those people who were close to you knew about it and they just showed up. In general, family celebrations were not too common. I never had a birthday party, for example. There was no Father's Day and no Mother's Day. We didn't need a special day to show our love and appreciation of our parents because we were a very close-knit family and, in that sense, every day was "Father's Day" or "Mother's Day."

When we came home Friday evening from the *beis midrash*, we made kiddush and had our meal. We sang *zemiros* (sabbath songs) at the table between the courses. We lived in the main Jewish area. There were no Conservative or Reform Jews. Everyone was either traditional or not observant at all. We never went to the *chassidische rebbes*, though there were quite a few in the community, since my father was what you might call "a *chassidische misnaged*" (member of a Lithuanian group opposed to the Hasidim). To put it simply, he did not believe that you needed a middleman, like a *rebbe*, to pray to God for you.

I joined Hashomer Hatzair at the age of twelve, in part, because I liked the atmosphere. People sang and danced and seemed both friendly and involved. Hashomer Hatzair rented an apartment in my father's house where they met. It was called a *ken*, literally, a bird's nest. They had a library, too, the second largest Jewish library in Radom, a city which had many such libraries.

Some of my old friends went to the cafes but I didn't hang out there. I identified closely with the working man from the earliest days of my youth and our kind of people didn't hang out in cafes. I always felt that the workers, what you might call "the simple people," had a better value system. They cared more about each other, they were more loyal to each other, and they were more sincere. Later on, at Buchenwald, I saw how such people helped others, while most of the intellectuals, who were soft and had never known hardship, did not.

I look back fondly upon those years in the movement. It was an exciting time to be an idealistic youth. We struggled with the big issues of the time for the Jewish people and mankind in general. And yet we managed to have a good time all the while.

We did everything as a group. We put on plays, most of which were standards of the Yiddish stage. I had parts in *Tevye, the Milkman, Yosef and his Brothers, God of Revenge, Between Day and Night,* and *Shulamit.* We also published our own newspaper, and contributed articles for the movement's Hebrew language paper which came out of Warsaw.

A favorite form of entertainment was scrambled newspaper readings. As a joke we'd mix up the topics. Two people would read from different newspapers, interweaving the articles. It sounded something like this:

Reader One: President Coolidge went to the White House.
Reader Two: ...and he decided to go to the *mikva* with his *chasidim* first.
Reader One: ...and then he gave a speech in the U.S. Senate.
Reader Two: ...but he had to leave in the middle to go to *minyan.*

As a devout Jew, my father did not approve of Hashomer Hatzair, which was ideologically antireligious. However, he saw that belonging to the organization was important to me and so he did not voice any objections to my joining. I guess he wanted me to be happy and he saw that this was what I wanted. On the other hand, although I wasn't observant, I knew that religion meant a great deal to him. Therefore, I continued attending services regularly even though I was no longer religious.

On Lag Ba'omer those of us in Hashomer Hatzair marched to Antoniowka, outside of Radom, built tents for the day, and played all sorts of games. In the evening we built campfires, and sang songs about our own Jewish country as we danced around the flames. I also immersed myself in books about the history and geography of Palestine and wrote for the monthly newspaper. A whole new world had opened up for me and I loved every minute of it. Together with my friends, we dreamed about returning to our ancient and beloved homeland. Helping to rebuild it became an obsession for us.

There was also a Hashomer Hatzair summer camp located about five hours from Radom by train, in the Carpathian Mountains. At first, I was the leader of a group, or *kevutzah*. Then, not long after, I was promoted, so to speak, and became head of a *gdud*, which was made up of several *kevutzot*. We lived in tents. Each *gdud* had its own flag and each *gdud* member wore its unique scarf. We also wore special khaki-colored scout hats with a large brim.

My plan was to make *aliyah*, emigrating to Palestine with my group. In order to prepare for physical labor and communal living, we went on *hachsharah* (preparation) for six months. I worked in a plywood factory near the village of Ostrolenka, close to the Russian border. Conditions were tough, but we were determined to persevere. Mordechai Weisman, one of my closest friends, got an infection from a splinter and died in the hospital. My father sent me food packages which I refused to accept due to my ideological commitment. We were living as a collective community and no individual was entitled to more than his comrades.

In 1933, I decided it was time to make *aliyah*. I was nineteen years old then. We felt that Jews shouldn't only be tradesmen, but that we should build a homeland with workers and farmers and become a nation just like the other nations of the world. But to make *aliyah* meant obtaining certificates for entry to Palestine from the British. Only a few were available for our group. The Hashomer Hatzair chapter in each town received its share of certificates according to the number of Hashomer Hatzair members it had. There were maybe thirty people on the waiting list in Radom and priority was given to those who were less well off. Married people also received preference because a couple could go on one certificate. In some cases a young man and a young woman would get married fictitiously so that they could share a certificate.

It was at this time that I met Rachel Weintraub. She was a charming beauty who belonged to another *gdud*, and she was just as devoted to Zionist goals as I was. We began spending a lot of time together, sharing our dreams and hopes for the future. Eventually, we fell in love and got married in 1937. We readied ourselves to emigrate to Palestine, and the day finally arrived when I had to tell my father of our imminent departure. He looked at me and, as was his way, he conveyed his thoughts without saying a word. His message was clear. The sadness in his face expressed his pain in losing his youngest child to a far-off land. So, out of consideration for his feelings, we postponed our plans.

A year later, in 1938, our daughter, Emma, was born. We still wanted to make *aliyah*, even as we started to create a life for ourselves in Radom.

My immediate concern was to find a way to support my young family. My father wanted me to join the family business. But two of my brothers were already in it and they too had families to support. I didn't think the business could sustain any more families. My father helped me open up another store, a few blocks away, which catered to the needle trade. We sold furs and textiles. I took into this venture my brother Moishe's brother-in-law, Nathan, as a partner, because of his expertise in textiles. He was given a 20 percent interest in the store without any investment on his part because we believed we could rely on him and because we wanted him to have a vested interest in the concern.

Rachel and I continued to receive encouraging letters from our friends in Palestine telling us how happy they were. I still have friends living today on Kibbutz Mishmar Ha-Emek, where most of our group settled. Had the war not intervened, I am certain that we would have one day fulfilled our dream of joining our comrades.

Most Polish Jews professed a love for Palestine, but did not see it as a realistic alternative to life in Poland. Although we had to face relentless anti-Semitism, second class citizenship and economic hardship, few were willing to leave their families and communities behind in Poland. And yet, we were truly a nation apart from the Polish nation. The 1,000 years that Jews lived in Poland were not long enough for us to become full citizens. Even our language was different. Our primary language was Yiddish, and most Jews spoke Polish with an accent Poles could easily detect. While some Jews joined the Polish Army, most did their best to avoid it. The officers and soldiers were very anti-Semitic and often made fun of how the Jews didn't know how to use a rifle, handle ammunition, or speak Polish well. Many who faced the draft under such circumstances sought all kinds of devices to avoid military service. Some found ways to lose weight, others put sand in their eyes. I also had no interest in serving in the Polish Army. Already somewhat overweight, I asked our doctor for advice. He suggested increasing my daily intake of food and recommended a certain diet. In addition, I went to a vacation resort known for helping people gain weight and it worked. When the army doctors examined me I was excused and told to come back in a year. When I returned, I had gained even more weight, so I was placed in the category known as "to be drafted only in case of war."

In 1939, when the war broke out, I was on a business trip in Vilna. Things were very chaotic and it was difficult to return to Radom. Train service was interrupted, and it was only possible to travel by truck. If I had stayed in Vilna, I probably would have made it safely through the war, since it was possible to travel from Vilna on to Shanghai, where many Jews found a safe haven throughout the war period. I returned to Radom because I didn't want to leave my family and because I was afraid that the authorities would consider me a deserter. I had no idea it would be such a short war for Poland. When I reported to the Army I was put in charge of giving out uniforms, shoes, etc., to the soldiers at the Sadkow Airfield on the outskirts of Radom. The war had begun on a Friday. By Wednesday, five days later, the government in Radom had collapsed and all the officials had left the town. So my brother came to see me at the airfield and said: "Why are you standing here in uniform? The war is almost over." When I heard that, I left the airfield and returned home. Two days later, the Germans marched into Radom. They were now in command.

Prior to the war, the thought of fleeing Poland to evade the Germans never entered our minds. We had no idea there would be a Holocaust. True, there had been pogroms over the years but these almost always lasted a brief time. It was impossible to conceive of a situation where a madman and people of a presumably cultured nation would methodically kill millions of Jews. That's why, when my brother Mannes wrote to us about coming to America, we weren't even interested. We had our own lives in Radom. Besides I had never met Mannes because he had left Poland before I was born.

Soon, I would be arrested, and I would never see Radom again as I remember it. The Jewish community and its flourishing Jewish culture were destroyed. Most of the Jewish inhabitants of Radom would be murdered, with a handful of survivors scattered to the far corners of the earth. Their faces remain vividly alive in my memory, but for the rest of humanity they are just lumped together into the "six million" figure. What is six million? When you look at that number you see merely a six followed by six zeros. You don't see parents and children. You don't see rabbis, professionals, and workers. You don't see teachers and eager students. You don't see communal and cultural institutions which took hundreds of years to develop. "Six million" is just too anonymous a term to convey what was really lost during the Holocaust.

Let me give you just a couple of examples from the multitude to try to provide some human dimension to the "six million." My mother's brother, Uncle Zysel, had two brilliant and talented sons. One, Chaim Nuchym, played the violin like a Yehudi Menuhin. To learn how to read music, he would sneak out without his father's knowledge to study with a local church organist. The oldest, Rachmil, was an artist who could draw your picture like a photograph after looking at you for just a short time. Neither of them survived the war. It is impossible to calculate how many talented people like these were lost to the Jewish community because of the Holocaust.

My father's sister, Salcia, was an actress and the black sheep of our family. She left Radom for Warsaw to find employment when the family was very poor. While there, she became interested in acting, went to drama school, and eventually became a very well known actress. As a result, the family sat *shiva* for her. Aunt Salcia was like a *shanda* (shame) for the family. She was very famous in Europe; she performed in Paris, London, and other major European cities. She made a lot of money and enjoyed a lavish life-style. Then, when she got older and was no longer an actress, she married and, together with her husband, opened a restaurant in Poznan.

Some time after that, Aunt Salcia lost her money and ended up operating a laundry in a resort town, Inowroclaw, that was not far from Poznan. Twice a year she came to us to commemorate her parents' *yahrzeit*. She wore old furs that had been bought in the days when she was better off. Now, of course, they were all dried-out. Sadly, she was unable to accept this forced change in her life-style and continued to play the role of a rich lady. But what we remembered in particular was the fact that even though she had become poor, she continued to bring us nice presents. We learned about her true situation because one day, on our way to Gdansk, my brother and I dropped in on her unexpectedly and found her washing other peoples' clothes by hand and wringing them out in a bathtub. She felt embarrassed even though we told her it didn't matter to us what she was doing. In truth, we were quite shocked to see her in this condition. Not long after that, the war broke out and we never saw her again. I can only presume that she suffered the same fate as millions of other Jews.

My sister, Chana Roiza, who lived in Kozienice was an early victim of the war. She and five of her nine children were killed by a German Luftwaffe bomb in the very first days of the war. The only bomb to hit the city landed on their apartment building. One of her sons, Sidney Lipman, happened not to be in the apartment at the time. His father, Avraham, had sent him to buy tobacco in the store and so Sidney wasn't there when the bomb hit. When he returned, the house was gone, replaced by a huge crater. All that was left was part of a wall of Sidney's uncle's apartment. Chana Roiza and her children were among the last family members to receive a proper Jewish burial during the war. The other family members who survived the bombing were eventually killed during the Holocaust. Their ashes are commingled with those of six million others. Only Sidney, out of a family of eleven, survived the war. Today he has a family and lives in Queens.

2

The Beginning of the End:
Arrest and Deportation

The German Army entered Radom on Friday, September 8, 1939. Rumors were rampant that the Germans needed workers for their factories in the Fatherland, and that there would soon be roundups of young Jewish men. A number of Jews, fearing the worst, left Radom two days before the Germans came in. We, too, almost left for Russia. We began to pack our belongings, putting things in the wagon. How I wish we had! But then we started to think: "How can we just leave everything?" Only a small part of our possessions, accumulated through the years, would even have fit into the wagon. And so we decided to stay.

Contrary to the rumors, the regular army soldiers behaved very nicely at first. Their goal was to fool the people into reopening their shops by making them feel secure. They gave big tips to the barbers, even larger than the cost of the haircut itself. Poor people who had no food in their homes sent out their children to sell toothbrushes, combs, pencils, and other items. The Germans paid the children well for what they were selling and were very friendly to them. They issued proclamations telling us to report any soldier who acted improperly by robbing or stealing from the local inhabitants. The older people remembered how nice the Germans were during the First World War and so pretty soon they began to take out the goods from where they had hidden them, just as the Germans wanted. Meanwhile, the Germans paid the full price for everything that they bought in the stores.

When I think about it, maybe the Jews should have known better because about three years before the war we began to see more ethnic Germans, *Volks-Deutsche*, in Poland. These people, as well as Poles who agreed with them, began posting slogans not to buy from Jews and blackmailing those who went into Jewish-owned stores. They also printed lists and published photographs in their newspapers of Gentiles who bought from Jews. Maybe we didn't notice so much what was going on because certain trades were completely controlled by Jews anyway. For example, our business, furs, was a totally Jewish trade and we weren't affected by these boycotts.

We were concerned that money might not be as valuable as items like leather or textiles. Nathan, whom I had taken in as a minor partner, suggested to me that we use our savings to purchase leather and hide it for safekeeping under the steps in my house. We did so and felt secure in our decision.

However, things changed pretty quickly. It seemed that almost overnight, the Wehrmacht, the German Army, was replaced by Hitler's Storm Troopers, the SS, who stole, robbed, and beat the citizens indiscriminately. They stopped paying for everything. In fact, they came in trucks, loaded them with goods, and paid nothing for them. Afraid that the Germans would somehow learn about the leather, I asked Nathan to remove his portion from our hiding place, which he did. I then proceeded to sell my share.

In Radom there was a man named Brenner, who had been deported from Germany a year before as an *Ostjüde*. People felt sorry for him at first, and generally made him feel welcome. But he turned out to be a traitor and an informer for the Nazis. By acting friendly towards everyone he was able to get invited to many peoples' homes, including our own. In this way he was able to learn who had money and who didn't, who was politically active and who wasn't, and so on. Brenner also became a good friend of Nathan. Like many others, Nathan divulged quite a bit about his financial dealings to Brenner as well as those of the rest of our family. Nathan was flattered by Brenner's friendship and got involved in some of his schemes. What Nathan didn't know was that Brenner was also having an affair with his pretty wife.

Nathan began to ask me for loans. I gave him money on several occasions, but when I saw that he wasn't paying me back, I realized that this was simple extortion. As a result, I stopped giving him money. Unbeknownst to me, my father continued to make payments to Nathan, fearing that he would betray us to the SS. When my father finally put an end to the blackmail, Nathan became angry and told Brenner that I had hidden leather in my house. Brenner related this information to the Gestapo. However, when the Nazis came to the house and tore up the floorboards, they were unable to find the merchandise because I had already sold it. They cursed me and left in disgust. As we shall see, this did not prevent Nathan and Brenner from trying to hurt me in other ways.

The Germans began a systematic effort to slowly degrade and humiliate us and to weaken our will to resist—in short, to break our spirit. For example, they would force two elderly Jews to climb trees and order them to call out "Cuckoo!" over and over again to each other, like two birds. At random, the Germans would cut off the beards of Jews they found in the street, often shearing off the flesh of their chins along with the hair.

The Nazis confiscated an apartment house complex near the ammunition factory in town, and forced out all of the Polish tenants. They rounded up Jews to clean the apartments and wash the windows for them. While they were doing so, the Germans frequently hurled their Jewish victims out the windows to their deaths. At first, people were outraged by all of the savagery, but little by little, they began to accept it as a part of life.

Shortly thereafter, people began to be pulled off the street and out of their own houses and put to work. The "work," was not really for any purpose, other than to torture the people.

One day I too, was grabbed off the street and taken, along with other Jews, to the courtyard of the *Shulkult*, a local Jewish school. There, the Nazis began playing a diabolical game with us. An SS man ate an apple and then he gave the core to one of us to finish.

After the man had reluctantly put it in his mouth, the Nazi would say to him: "You *schweinhund!* You're eating from the other fellow's mouth," and would hit him. After that, the Jew would be told to give the core to the next person. Seeing what had happened to the first one, this fellow would throw the core into the gutter. But when he did so he too was beaten. "You're making the street dirty," they would say. From this I learned that you could be hit for eating the apple core or for throwing it away. So when my turn came, I put the core in my pocket. This turned out to be the right move.

A few minutes later they found another excuse for beating us some more. A German asked us what our occupations were. When he heard that I was a furrier he ordered me to make a vest for him. Playing for time, I started taking measurements, using a piece of string. A few minutes later the one who had asked me to do this began hitting me. Apparently he had forgotten that he had asked me to work on the vest. To distract him, I said: "Sir, perhaps you would like a jacket with sleeves instead of a vest? I have to measure the length of the sleeves; do you want it with sleeves or without sleeves?" He barked back that he wanted sleeves and then turned away to beat up some other people. Then he came back and asked me when the jacket would be ready. I told him it would take three days but he didn't believe me. He thought he wouldn't be able to find me then so he made me take him to my house.

A few days later he showed up at my door without any warning. I was taking a shave and singing when he walked in and said: "Furrier, you come with me." I was afraid to go with him but I had no choice. I was taken in a long black automobile to a building that originally had been used as a lodging for munitions workers and that had now been converted into a German warehouse, with offices and storerooms. I was brought into a room filled with blankets and other items that they wanted me to preserve, to put in camphor. This was indeed work customarily done by furriers. Since they needed furriers they ordered me to come in again the next day. They were already thinking about invading Russia and they wanted warm clothing for the soldiers.

I was afraid to go to the warehouse by myself and felt it would be safer to work there with a few people. So I told the Germans I needed help to fulfill the order. They agreed and I asked some of the residents in our apartment building to come along, offering to pay them myself for each day's labor. Times were very hard and people were desperate, so a number of them eagerly accepted, despite their fear of the Nazis.

The Germans called me to work a number of times. Every time I finished a job the cashier paid me a substantial sum, which I then divided among the workers. For them, in these hard times, the money was very welcome and pretty soon, instead of being afraid to work for the Germans, the workers would ask me: "When are we going again?"

One day, the SS brought me to the usual place to estimate the number of people I would need for a new job. Instead of sending me towards the right, as they normally did, they suddenly pointed left and ordered me into a large, empty room. The furniture consisted of nothing more than a desk and a chair. Along the walls, at intervals, were four or five doors.

I felt that something was very wrong and, as it turned out, I was right. Within a minute all of the doors opened. SS men carrying sticks or canes came charging through each door. They began hitting me almost immediately. The officer who generally picked me up for work was also there, yet he acted with the same cruelty as the others.

"Where have you hidden the furs?" they demanded. I was shown a typewritten statement signed by Nathan, the man in whom I had once placed my trust. It consisted of an accusation that I had hidden furs in my house and that I had also held pro-communist, anti-Nazi meetings in our store. It seems that they were charging me with being both a capitalist and a communist!

I denied all their accusations, but they didn't care. They bent me over the chair with my head under the desk and they proceeded to beat me so badly that I lost consciousness. To revive me, I was tossed into a bathtub with cold water. This had the desired effect but at that point I was bleeding so badly that when I eventually came to, I couldn't open my eyes. I was thrown into a truck and taken to prison.

The jail had a little hospital room. My family was able to bribe certain officials and have me transferred to it. A doctor was sent to treat me. My brother and other family members smuggled letters into the prison to keep my spirits up. They wrote that I shouldn't lose hope because the Judenrat had promised that I would be freed very soon.

In the jail ten to twelve people had to share one cell. Usually, we slept on the floor because there weren't enough cots. They didn't give us much food, but even if they had, I wouldn't have eaten because I had no appetite. My family sent in some delicacies but I was unable to eat them. I was able, however, to buy protection from some of the more violent prisoners with the cigarettes they smuggled in to me.

One morning a package from home was brought to my prison cell. In it was a pillow and some warm, long underwear, as well as a picture of my little baby daughter. To me this could only mean that my family had learned that I was going to be sent away. And so it was. All my hopes of being released were dashed.

That very evening, all of us were brought into the prison courtyard. In front of us stood a German officer who told us: "You're all going to Germany, where you'll become good, honest people and true workers." At 3:00 A.M., accompanied by blows from rifle butts and rubber truncheons, we were marched off to the railroad station and put on a freight train. All in all, there were about 200 of us, mostly Christian Poles. We could not have imagined in our wildest dreams, or nightmares even, what lay in store for us.

We rode for hours and the train made many stops, adding more people along the way as well as additional cars to accommodate them. After one day's travel we arrived in Lodz. The train stopped at a railroad siding on the outskirts of the city and about thirty of us were taken to an abandoned factory used as a prison and guarded by SS soldiers.

The following night we were awakened by a loud banging on the door. We jumped up, covered with straw. We had no need to get dressed because we had never gotten undressed. The Germans chased us out to the accompaniment of blows with rifle butts to a waiting truck. They told us: "You are the Death Commando," meaning that we were assigned to a unit to bury the dead. We rode for about half an hour until we came to a wooded area. There we were ordered to take heavy shovels from the truck and were forced to run through the woods as the Germans beat us again.

In a few minutes we came to an open clearing where we saw a horrible sight. A ditch about thirty feet long was filled with dead, torn bodies. They belonged to Jews who had been blown up with hand grenades after having been forced to dig their own graves. I was shocked and my eyes filled with tears. "Fill up the ditch with earth!" came the order by the Germans. Some people were completely numb with fear and didn't move right away. These poor souls were shoved into the ditch and we were forced to cover them too. After we had finished, we were taken back to the factory.

They forced us to perform this ghoulish task for several nights in a row. It was an unbelievably horrifying experience. We had to pick up mangled corpses, pieces of bone and flesh, and broken skulls that were lying nearby, and throw them into the ditches. All this was but a small taste of things to come. Even so I will never forget this first encounter with brutality as long as I live.

Embarking again on the train, we rode until we came to Zbonszyn, a town on the German border. On each of the boxcars in which we rode was written in large letters the city from which those in it came.

In this way the SS man who had originally ordered me to make him a vest was able to find me. He remembered that when he forced his way into my apartment, I was singing while I was shaving. To make fun of me, he wanted me to perform for his fellow soldiers. I was told to stand on a bench at the platform and sing Polish songs. I was so nervous and traumatized by my experience in Lodz that I couldn't utter a sound. Disgusted, he hit me several times and chased me back to the boxcar.

The following day we arrived at Weimar, Germany, where we waited in the cars for ten hours without any food or water. Then, around midnight, the doors were flung open and the SS, accompanied by large black dogs, screamed at us to jump out onto the ground. Stunned and disoriented, some of the deportees lost their balance and fell. They were immediately removed and put on trucks, never to be seen again.

As for the rest of us, we began the tortuous five miles march to Buchenwald, a place which was to change my life forever.[1]

Note

1. The camp was given the name, Buchenwald, on July 28, 1937, by Heinrich Himmler.

3

Buchenwald: The First Few Months

I remember that when I first came to the camp after our exhausting and terrible march from the train station I was in shock. People were marching and running around in striped uniforms that resembled pajamas. I had never seen anything remotely like this before. In terms of the chaos and the constant motion of the inmates it reminded me of a three-ring circus. No one gave us any idea as to how long we would be there, but we didn't think we'd come out alive. It was as if we had been deposited on another planet. I felt that after this I wouldn't go to hell anymore because I was already there. In those early days, in 1939, Germany seemed all-powerful and we didn't expect the Germans to lose.

Our transport contained the last Jewish group of any size that entered the camp until 1944, perhaps 150 to 200 Jews out of two transports numbering a total of 3,200 deportees. The Jews were chosen at random, but among the Gentiles there were many political leaders. This was done, apparently, to frighten the local populace into cooperating with the Nazi occupiers. Isolated as we were, we knew nothing about gas chambers as a method of mass extermination until late in the war. Buchenwald did not even have a crematorium until 1940. Until then the bodies of those who died, whether from beatings, shootings, hunger or illness were carted off to the crematorium in Weimar for efficient disposal. Incidentally, it is hard to imagine that the local townsfolk didn't question where all the bodies were coming from.

Initially, we were put in a tent camp, *zeltlager*, one of five such tents, surrounded by thick barbed wire. It was located within the

33

area of Buchenwald known as "The Small Camp" or *kleinelager*, which was often used to quarantine the prisoners upon their arrival. We remained there for three months. During this period we did no work, spending our days talking and just sitting around. We were like the homeless people who lie in the streets all day. At night, we slept on the ground. We each had less than a foot of space and we always woke up with sores. For us this was all very worrisome for we realized that if we were of no use to the Nazis, not even as laborers, then we would soon be put to death. Every morning we discovered dozens of people scattered about the camp who had died at night from hunger, dysentery, whatever. Even if they were alive it didn't matter. Whoever couldn't move was taken away and killed.

Our daily diet consisted of a little soup, which was really water, and a slice of bread. Sometimes, the people who brought the bread in showed us pieces of ground glass that were in it. When you held it up, it shone like diamonds. In this way, they could slowly kill us by cutting out our insides. I wondered why they didn't simply kill us right away. Perhaps it was cheaper this way. Sometimes we were also given *ersatz*, or substitute coffee, that was poisoned. In those first few weeks, I hardly ate anything because I was still in a state of shock.

We wore the same clothes during this period and we were infested with lice, so one can imagine how we looked. During the three months that I was in the tent camp I lived in the same suit that I'd come in with. I wore it as I lay on the muddy ground. We slept on wooden planks and the mud oozed out and practically covered us. Whenever possible, we washed ourselves with snow that had collected on the ground. The winter climate was terrible and it was not unusual for the temperatures to go below zero degrees fahrenheit.

About midway through my stay in the Small Camp, the Nazis summoned me to headquarters. There they told me to make myself ready because I was being freed. Naturally, I was very excited when I heard this news. I had heard in the camp that shortly before the war, many Jews and non-Jews who had visas to America were let go. So naturally, when they told me I was leaving, I thought that I too would be released. When I returned to the camp, several Underground leaders approached me and asked that I tell the outside world the truth about the horrors of Buchenwald. I was given names and addresses of a few important people to contact. I memorized this information as best as I could since it would have been too dangerous to write it down.

The whole thing, however, turned out to be a hoax and yet another example of Nazi sadism. Just as I was ready to leave for home, I was suddenly given a hard kick in my back. "*Schweinehund,* go back to the *zeltlager!*" the guard screamed. "You'll never get out of here alive!" This revelation was the sharpest blow I had yet received. It took quite some time for me to pull myself out of the resulting depression.

We were both relieved and nervous about the future when our transport was taken out of the tent camp in March of 1940 and given permanent housing in wooden barracks where we joined other prisoners. We would be allowed to live, it seemed, but for how long and under what conditions, no one knew. The conditions in the tent camp had taken a terrible toll. Most of those who had come in with me were dead. After we left, the tent camp was destroyed.

We were required to remove all of our clothes and put them in individual burlap bags. At this time I still had my suit, shirt, shoes, and socks, but everything was filthy and soiled, almost beyond recognition, because I had, like everyone else, been wearing these same items for about three months.

Next, the barbers removed all of our body hair, not with a shaver, but with a clipper. Our hair was cut short, but, using a razor, they completely removed a small strip of hair running the length of our heads in the center. We were left with a small strip of bare skin which they mockingly called the "Street of the Lice." I felt like a sheep must feel when it's shorn. The hair that had been removed was placed in sacks for future use.

We were then chased into the showers. The water, however, was very hot, and many people, perhaps half of those in the group, were unable, in their weakened condition, to stand it, and died from the severe shock. Perhaps this was just another means intended by the Nazis to weed out the weak. Then they ordered us to step into a vat filled with a disinfectant that burned like fire. When we emerged naked, with no hair, and dripping wet, we looked so much like skeletons that we couldn't recognize each other. Instead of a stomach, there was a hole. In any case, by the end of this process only 160 or so people remained out of the 3200 in my transport.

From there we were required to run naked at full speed to the clothing distribution center in the bitter cold. We were issued our prison garb without regard to size. A tall man could be given short pants and a short man long pants. *"Hollander"* wooden shoes were given out and they were frequently either too small or too big, and so on. Sometimes people would get stuck in the mud with these clogs and we'd have to help them out. Naturally, we tried to even matters out by exchanging the various items amongst ourselves. Finally, we were given numbers—I got #7197—to sew into our clothing, and chased into a barrack. These numbers became, in effect, our names. We were frequently asked to call off our numbers and if we forgot, they beat us. In addition, I was given a red triangle, indicating that I was a political prisoner, and a yellow triangle, indicating that I was a Jew. They were sewn together, the yellow pointing up and the red one over it pointing down, forming a Jewish star. Inside the red triangle was the letter "P" for Polish.

I was assigned to Block 28, which had originally been built for prominent German political leaders who had been sent to the camp. Now it had become a barrack for Jews only. It was approximately 175 feet by 25 feet. It had two wings, an A Wing and a B Wing. In the middle there was a washroom. Each wing had an eating room and a sleeping room. Each eating table had two benches and we sat ten on each side. If anyone died during the day, they were replaced in the evening because every table had to have 21 people. At the head of our table sat the *tischalteste* (person in charge of food), Professor Heinemann, who had been on the faculty of a German university before the war. He was a *mischlinge* (person of mixed race) who hated Jews; his grandfather had been a Jew, but his son was already "pure" enough to become a Nazi. The Nazis considered Heinemann a Jew and, in a way, it was very sad. I remember how one Christmas he made himself a candle for the holiday, mixing margarine and clay together. He then pulled out a thread from his jacket to use as a wick. He took out of his pocket a small twig, maybe five inches long, which he had snapped off of a branch of a tree. And then he just sat there, staring at the little flame and his small Christmas tree, crying bitterly.

Next to each table was a cabinet, seven feet high, three feet wide, divided into 21 cubbies. In each cubby was a wooden board to cut the bread. On it was a red and white checkerboard cloth napkin. On top was an aluminum bowl, inside it an aluminum coffee cup with a handle, and on the right side a knife, a fork, and a spoon. It was basically for the benefit of the Red Cross, in case they came and inspected. Every Wednesday, an SS man came with a pin, which he stuck into the aluminum handles of the bowl to see if it was perfectly clean. It was called the *geshier-appel* (dishes detail). And if it wasn't perfectly clean, the *stubedienst* (barrack orderly) was often beaten and, in some cases, even killed. It was unbelievable. They had a world war going on and they sent people to check on how clean our bowls were! I had no money, so I sold my margarine for a few *pfennig* and bought toothpaste from the canteen, when it was available, not to clean my teeth, but to make my dishes shine. No one used any of these items because if you did and they were not spotlessly clean, you could lose your life. We tried to eat from cans or whatever we could improvise, anything to avoid eating from these bowls, because we were afraid to get them dirty.

In the evening, prisoners were sent out to bring the food from the kitchen. Generally, this consisted of barrels of a yellowish soup made from the remains of turnips that had been given to animals. It was very important to stir the soup so that everyone would get a fair portion. Otherwise, the water was on top and the "good stuff" would be at the bottom. On Sunday, in the daytime, around 1:00 P.M. we were given rotten potatoes with the skin on them. And once a year, on Hitler's birthday, we were treated to a hot chocolate.

Every morning, while it was still dark, 5:00 A.M. in the winter and 4:00 A.M. in the summer, we were awakened to the sound of a whistle and the greeting of: "*Schweinhunds*! Get up!" Nobody was late and no one said they didn't feel well, because they were afraid to do so. In fact, when we had roll call, the dead had to be there, along with the living. This was because no one was officially declared dead until the end of the evening roll call.

After receiving a slice of bread and the black hot water, which we called coffee, we were chased out of the barracks for the morning roll call. It was still dark as we moved out to begin the day. Long columns of men dragged themselves down the roads lethargically, clearly resigned to their fate—the legions of the damned.

In the morning everything went faster because they wanted the inmates to begin working as soon as possible. At the *appelplatz* (assembly place) we were lined up five across according to our barracks. The *blockaltester* (block leader) of each barrack counted off his men until he was satisfied that everyone was present and then waited for the *scharführer* (officer). The large square was overcrowded with prisoners. In the winter it was bitterly cold and the wind literally whistled through our clothes. Most of the men were silent as they stood except for the sudden whispered warning of "Look out!" as the *scharführer* approached.

At that point the *blockaltester* called out: "Block 28, eyes left!" The *blockaltester* walked towards the *scharführer*, pulled the cap from his head, stood at attention, and gave his report. The *scharführer* walked to the head of the column that had been formed by our block and snarled: "Count off!" While the counting proceeded, like clockwork, from row to row, the *scharführer* moved quickly through the lines to make sure the rows were complete. After this, the *blockaltester* called out: "At ease." At that point, the men, who had stood perfectly still throughout this entire procedure, relaxed visibly. Feet were stamped, hands rubbed, and arms swung. The men stood like this for nearly an hour on the square, as the sky became lighter and our limbs progressively stiffer. We breathed on our hands and rubbed our noses and ears to keep them warm. Then, finally, an announcement was made over the loudspeakers: *"Arbeits commandos antraten!"* ("Work commandos report!").

We were led by a prisoner wearing an armlet with the word *"kapo"* on it. Shortly before reaching the gate a command came to pull our caps from our heads. We were warned to march in step as we went through the gate. Anyone who failed to do so could expect the worst. He was lucky if he received only a few blows from a rifle butt. More often than not, the punishment was twenty-five lashes. As we marched to the beat of songs played poorly by the camp band at the gate, we were sent out to work to the accompaniment of a few more blows delivered by our tormentors.

Ilse Koch was the commandant's wife, but she was also a commandant herself. Whenever we saw her we trembled with fear. She waited at the gate on a white horse every morning as we left the camp, right by the sign: *"Recht Oder Unrecht, Unser Vaterland"* ("Right or Wrong, Our Fatherland"). On the gate itself was the sign: *"Jedem Das Seine"* ("To Each His Just Reward"). Often she would select, at random, people to be killed. If anyone displeased her, she wrote down their number. For example, if she thought someone was staring at her, his number was noted. Even though Buchenwald was a concentration camp only for male prisoners, who was interested in looking at a woman under these conditions? And in any case, she was actually quite an ugly woman, and in our eyes a monster.[1] At the evening roll call they would call out the numbers that she had taken down. These people never returned.

In general, you couldn't hide, not from her, nor from anyone else. Every SS man knew every prisoner's history just by looking at the triangle they wore. Political prisoners had red, criminals had green, homosexuals a pink one, antisocials like vagrants or the chronically unemployed wore black, and Jehovah's Witnesses, a purple triangle. Royal blue triangles were worn by those captured in other countries fleeing the German onslaught. All prisoners, except for Germans, had the first letter of the name of their country of origin stamped in the middle of their triangle. A Jew, no matter what else he was, had to have a yellow triangle pointing upwards, in addition to whatever other identifying triangle he had. Together they formed a Star of David. If a Jew was a political prisoner, as I was, he had a red triangle facing downward, a yellow triangle facing upward, and, say, a "P" that stood for Poland.

Actually, we had little direct contact with the SS. They had organized the camp so that it could be run efficiently with a minimum of guards. Orders were passed on and enforced by inmate functionaries. We were afraid to talk to the SS officers directly because other inmates might then accuse us of being collaborators. The SS officers didn't talk to us either, except to curse at us.

When we returned from work outside the camp, we had to stop by the pile of stones next to the quarry and carry one back to the camp. We had to quickly grab a sufficiently large stone in order to avoid being beaten.

Before entering the barrack we used a brush and water from a bucket to clean off our shoes. We held them over a pan to catch the dirt. We were starving, but the camp's main concern was cleanliness! Therefore, if they didn't like the way you did it, they'd hit you and make you do it again.

In the bedroom there were three tiers of bunk beds. Actually, they looked more like wooden shelves. We had no mattress, only burlap wrapped straw pallets. After a while, the straw began to fall out. The Nazis were constantly looking for new ways to use the *stubediensts* to punish the prisoners. If they found even two or three pieces of loose straw on the floor, everyone was forced to sweep the floor on their knees for hours with toothbrushes. Afterwards, we were ordered to stand at attention while our tormentors inspected our toothbrushes. Naturally, since we were not given any time to clean them, the toothbrushes were dirty and we were punished yet again.

The sheets themselves were actually made of flannel. I usually slept in the middle tier. Not by choice. Nothing was by choice; we were assigned to our positions. Mine was the worst one because it was eye level. The top one was advantageous because they couldn't check it so well for neatness. But to get into it, you had to be an acrobat. Every week the blankets were put in piles of ten in the dining room. Sometimes, we never knew when, an SS man came to the barrack and counted them. If any were missing, the *stubedienst* was beaten up by the SS.

The rule was that when a *stubedienst* looked at the edge of the bunk beds, each one had to be as straight as a ruler. The Germans were fanatics about this requirement. If it wasn't straight the man in charge of the beds could be beaten to death by the SS. As a result, you can imagine how strict he was with the prisoners about it. Some people even gave away their bread to others in exchange for help with their beds because they weren't so good at making them.

We were given clean shirts every week and we had striped pants and jackets that we washed ourselves, usually on Sundays. But everything came with an order. You couldn't wash it when you wanted to, but only when they let you. Thus, if one's shirt got dirty, it might have to be worn that way for several days before it could be cleaned.

Once a week, usually on Sunday, we were able to take hot showers with soap. The soap was engraved "RJF." The *stubedienst* explained to us that the letters stood for *Reine Juden Fat*, meaning that fat from dead Jews was used to produce the soap. Even in the showers, the Nazis had to remind us of our ultimate fate.

Note

1. According to a British prisoner at Buchenwald, Ilse Koch was in the habit of identifying men whose appearance pleased her. These she invited to her room for sex, and later, to prevent them from talking, they were killed and disposed of in the crematorium. See Christopher Burney, *The Dungeon Democracy: What Became of European Civilization?* New York: Duell, Sloan & Pearce, 1946:11.

4

Working and Surviving

The stone quarry was the place with the worst working conditions and newcomers were often assigned there. That was my first job as well. Those selected for punishment were frequently sent to the quarry. It was common knowledge that working in the quarry meant almost certain death. The Polish group in which I arrived was nicknamed "The Snipers" and it was basically a punishment detail. In addition to our regular daytime work, we could be forced to perform other tasks at any time of night. For example, we might be ordered to unload trucks at two in the morning. Even though we weren't really snipers we were called that to justify their having arrested us. Targets were painted on the back of our coats, symbolizing the name we were given. This made us stand out and, as a result, we were often a target of additional brutality. People were killed in the quarry every single day without fail. A group of about 300 would leave in the morning, to the accompaniment of a band at the gate playing marching music, and perhaps 200 would return.

When I came back at the end of the day, I could scarcely believe that I was still alive. In part, I survived because I was afraid to cheat on the job. People who tried to cut corners were invariably caught because the supervision was so close. Also, I did my best never to fall when we marched to the quarry. If you did, it was a death sentence. It was really hard to avoid falling though, because the mud would get into our wooden shoes. We then had to try to scoop out the mud from inside the shoes without stopping or falling. And, of course, you had to be careful not to lose your shoes.

Anyone who did so was finished. Sometimes I fell inside the quarry itself, but luckily I survived that.

The work in the quarry was so hard that it would be fair to say that it was specifically designed to kill people. Certainly, we were disposable labor. If we died, we could always be replaced by an endless supply of slaves.

The labor was divided into different commandos (work details)—carrying the stones, breaking up the stones, and so on. Those assigned to breaking the stones were far more fortunate than the carriers. They were able to steal moments of rest in between the swings of their pickaxes. Dynamite was not used to reduce the stones to manageable size. The stone was stratified in layers only a couple of inches high, with numerous vertical fissures. This made it possible for a man to repeatedly shatter the stone into large chunks, day in and day out, using manual tools.

We were always hungry and wore only a single layer of clothing. Thus, we were ill equipped to perform strenuous physical labor in the cold. The howling, forceful winds of the Ettersberg Mountains pierced our bodies, spreading the cold through every fiber. It was a cold that we could never escape from until the start of summer. The wind threatened to throw us off balance with every step we took. My job was to carry a heavy stone up the 148 steps from the bottom of the quarry to the top of the excavation. There I threw it onto a pile of stones and then ran back down the quarry to start over once again.

Crucial to survival was learning how to select and hoist onto your shoulder the right stone in a split second. It took me about a week to master how to carry the stones. If you took a stone that was too small, they beat you up for being a loafer. And if you chose one that was too large, you ran the risk of collapsing under its weight. After a little while, I learned how to select stones that looked big but were lighter because they were a little hollow on the inside. The scene looked like something from Dante's *Inferno*—hundreds of emaciated human beings in striped uniforms digging and carrying, pulling rock-filled wagons out of a pit seven stories deep. All the while the hapless slaves were being pushed to their limits by Nazi officers who beat them with clubs, rifle butts, and tree branches on the slightest pretext, or perhaps none at all.

Every twenty feet a soldier, usually accompanied by a large dog, stood guard. All in all, there were, maybe, fifty guards. When people were killed at the quarry site, they were often simply thrown onto a pile of dead or half-dead bodies. Whenever a prisoner was killed, for whatever reason, the report always read: "Shot while trying to escape." Often, when the guards wanted to kill someone, they would deliberately force him over the "borderline" and then shoot the person for having "tried to get away." Sometimes, inmates who felt they could no longer stand the terrible conditions in the quarry would, in effect, commit suicide by intentionally stepping over the line.

Miraculously, I survived fourteen weeks in the quarry. I don't really know how. I certainly wasn't the strongest or the smartest. It was a record of sorts because most people lasted only 2 to 4 weeks. At one point during this period, my life was saved by a fortunate coincidence. After a particularly brutal beating, I was thrown, barely conscious, onto a pile of people, most of whom were already dead. They were ready to take us to a special barrack in the camp from where we would then be carted off to the crematorium in Weimar.

I don't know how long I lay there. I was numb and indifferent to my fate. I could hardly breathe because of the weight of the other bodies which were continually being flung on top of me. Every so often I heard terrible moaning from others who were also near death. Of course, no one paid the slightest attention to us. It made no difference to anyone whether we were alive or not. We were now destined to be burned in the crematorium.

As luck would have it, one of those who removed the bodies on stretchers was a man from my barrack, someone whose shoes I had polished in the past in return for his having given me some bread. Sometimes he had also allowed me to wash his bowl. This was actually a privilege since it gave me the opportunity to scrape out and eat whatever little food he might have left over. His name was Kolpak and he was a Jew from Vienna. Now, as I lay there, helpless, he recognized me and told his partner that I was still alive. His partner, to whom I was simply another body, was not sympathetic: "Forget about him; we have to take all these bodies back to the camp now for transfer to Weimar." They argued back and forth until, finally, Kolpak simply picked me up and carried me on his shoulders to the camp hospital, and that's how my life was saved.

By the time I came back to the quarry from the hospital, a rail had been laid. It went up the long ramp from the quarry to the public road which swung around the rim of the quarry. I spent the next four months as one of six so-called horses pushing lorries full of rocks up the metal tracks. Along the way, SS guards, using the butts of their rifles, and kapos, thrashing us with tree branches, prodded us to move faster. Once we reached our destination, we would tip the hinged lorry over, dumping the stones unto a pile. We then ran with the empty lorry down the hill, and filled it once again. Despite the pace and the beatings, pushing the wagon with others actually offered me some measure of relief when compared with having to carry a stone on my shoulder.

My next assignment was as a mason's helper in the *Bau* (Building) Commando. We built housing for the SS men. For six months, I carried stones, heavy cement bags, and other building materials. A load would be placed in a rectangular box with two poles on each side so that it could be carried by two prisoners. When we brought our load to the building site we were required to go up very steep wooden planks because there were no steps. Keeping our balance as we walked was almost impossible. As I look back, I don't know how we managed to do it, day in, day out.

The work was very difficult and it was made more unbearable by a particularly ill-tempered overseer. We had a German civilian building supervisor who used to try to catch us doing something wrong while we were carrying our loads or working on the scaffold. Often he hid and snuck up behind the work area, hoping to catch us as we took a short break. On the slightest pretext, he would beat us with an iron pipe. He came to a bad end, however. The SS caught him stealing building materials and made him a prisoner in Buchenwald, like the rest of us. His life was even more miserable than ours because the prisoners exacted their revenge by beating him up constantly. One day, he suffered an injury that required immediate medical attention. He was sent to the hospital where he was finished off.

To protect myself from the often freezing cold, I took an empty cement bag made out of paper and constructed a makeshift "vest." Alas, I was caught wearing it. My punishment for stealing Third Reich property was twenty-five lashes, each of which I had to count off out loud. I fainted after the first twelve. Not that it mattered; the inmate who assisted the SS man simply poured cold water on me and when I came to, they started over again from zero. As a result, the total number was thirty-seven lashes.

When they finished I was in terrible shape. The flesh on my back had been cut to ribbons and my body was literally drenched in blood. I was sent to the camp hospital with the intention of having the hospital staff complete the job and put an end to me. But thanks to Walter Kramer, who worked there and was a member of the Underground, I was given a *schoning*, an eight day recuperation period generally reserved for the sick. My bones ached so, that I needed every minute of rest I got and even that was not enough. Nevertheless, I recovered somewhat and there is no doubt that were it not for Kramer's action, I would surely have died a miserable death. Kramer, was considered a "surgeon" in the hospital, although he had been a metal worker by profession in his native Germany prior to the war.

After my discharge from the hospital, I returned to the *Bau* Commando. Gradually, I regained my strength and was able to resume working as I had been before this incident. As usual, I tried to avoid drawing attention to myself, but this was not always possible. On one occasion I was carrying a load together with my partner. We used a *trage*, a long rectangular box with two poles attached to the length of its sides. My partner was in front and I was in the rear as we started up a hill. The weight shifted in such a way that most of the load was on my end. A Nazi noticed this and began beating up my partner, calling him lazy for making me do most of the work. Then he ordered him to jump into a hole and told me to cover him with earth. I hesitated, even though I was very afraid to disobey. When you work with someone, they become like a brother to you. My failure to respond immediately, enraged the officer, who then told my partner to change places with me. However, he was also reluctant to do as he was told and, in frustration, the SS officer beat both of us and sent us back to work. We were extremely lucky not to have been executed on the spot.

Once, while I was in the Building Commando I was discovered taking a short break in a corner of a building. They reported me as a lazy person to the *scharführer*. I told him the cement bag had slipped and that I was trying to fix it. He then shouted out: "You *dreckische Jude*! You see this chimney? Tonight you're going up the chimney." And I, fed up with my miserable life in the camp, said to him: "I like it well-done." He enjoyed my response and started to laugh. This saved my life. He said to me: "Disappear from here" and I ran back to the Building Commando. Making a joke out of this may not have been the smartest thing to do, but it was my luck that in this instance my remark appealed to him.

Like everyone else, I was always trying to find ways to make our back-breaking work a little more bearable. I hit upon the idea of slipping a rope from the top of my shirt through both of my sleeves and looping it around the poles of the *trage*. In this way I would not have to grasp the poles with my hands all the time. Whenever my hands got tired, I could let go and have the rope do the work instead. While this was a definite improvement, it created another problem for me. After a while the rope would begin to irritate the skin near my shoulders. To relieve the pain of the rope burns, I once again resorted to the paper from an empty cement bag and put it between the rope and my shoulders. It should be understood that this paper wasn't needed in any way by the

Germans. It was thrown away after they took out the cement. Yet, as I had learned earlier, stealing the paper, Third Reich "property," was considered sabotage, and one could be punished very severely for it.

The rope and paper technique worked very well, but inevitably, I was caught, along with three other fellows who had followed suit. One of us was killed immediately. As for the rest of us, Otto Feuer, Karl Schnoog, and myself, we were hung in a fiendish manner. "You used this rope; you'll hang on a rope," said *Rapportfuhrer* Arnold Strippel. "And the whole camp will watch as you twist in the wind." Our hands were tied behind our backs and we were then suspended by our hands from a tree about two feet above the ground. With my feet hanging free, the weight of my whole body was on my shoulder joints and the pain was excruciating beyond description.

As I hung there I prayed for death to put an end to my misery. Finally, after several hours, I was cut loose from the tree. I would have died from the bleeding and the pain were it not for the Underground, which once again arranged to have me stay in the hospital for a week so that I could recuperate from my injuries.[1]

After my recovery, I was assigned to the *Fuhr Colonne* (Riding Commando). Six prisoners would wear harnesses attached together by a chain to a wagon we had to pull. Sometimes we were forced to sing the Buchenwald Song as we pulled, but mostly we sang the Thuringian Forest song because it had a faster beat and allowed our tormentors to increase the pace. For this reason we were mockingly called "the singing horses." In reality, however, our throats were so dry, especially when it was hot outside, that the singing sounded more like croaking. Occasionally, the foreman would count out loud: "One, two, three, four," in rapid succession to make us pull more quickly. Altogether, there were sixteen wagons. I was part of wagon number 5. Our load consisted of large heavy rocks, cement bags, and other heavy items. It wasn't easy to pull the wagon, especially since they beat us as we did our work.

There was one benefit to being a horse. At least when we arrived at our destination we didn't have to unload the wagon. Other people were used for that purpose. The German mentality was very rigid and in this instance, actually worked in our favor. Because we had been defined as horses we were not required to remove the materials, since, as they put it: "A horse cannot unload."

In October of 1941, a transport of Russian POWs arrived in Buchenwald. They were kept in isolation and we were not allowed to have any contact with them. The officers were selected and brought into the horse stables which had been set up for mass liquidation. The room was furnished like a doctor's office, with soft music being played in the background. It gave the impression of being a very peaceful place. No one suspected what was about to happen. The POWs were ordered to remove their shirts as if they were about to be examined by a doctor. They were told to stand on a device that looked like a cross between a subway turnstile and a doctor's scale, with two adjustable prongs that firmly gripped the head and pulled the victim up or down according to his height. When the person's neck reached the intended spot, a pointed iron rod pierced his throat. The contraption was called "Every Minute a Dead Person." If it failed to kill the prisoner immediately, the Nazis simply shot him. For some reason the Germans stopped using this machine after killing the Russian officers. After the war, the Americans found these machines intact, as well as the drawings used to build them.

After being killed, the POWs' bodies were thrown into trucks and taken to the crematorium. In the courtyard of the crematorium, gallows had been erected. They were used to hang people all through the remainder of the war. The road over which the trucks passed was called "The Street of Blood" because the blood from the dead Russian POWs' dripped onto it. Our wagon was assigned to remove the evidence before it would rile up the other inmates. Each night our wagon was loaded up with rock salt which was then sprayed over the icy road so that the blood would be absorbed and mix into the mud.

By the next morning, everything had melted and the bloodstains were completely covered and were no longer visible to anyone who walked on the road. The slaughter of the Russian POWs' continued for weeks, and so every night we had to repeat this task. They told us that if we opened our mouths about what we'd seen, we'd go up the chimney. To make it less likely that we would talk, we were kept away from other inmates during the daytime, and worked only at night.

Towards the end of this assignment, my leg became infected from sores caused by my wooden shoes. At first, I was afraid to go to the hospital, but eventually I had no choice. I could no longer walk, I was burning with fever, and it was the only hope I had of getting better, so I took my chances and went to the hospital. It was fortuitous that I did so. That very night the remaining "horses" of Wagon 5, along with the replacement who wore my harness, were ordered to pull the wagon to the quarry instead of to the stables. Contrary to the usual procedure, the wagon was empty. When they reached the quarry the men were told to remove their harnesses and were then executed on the spot. Since the Nazis had completed the job of killing the Russian soldiers, there was no longer a need to salt the road. They intended to tidy up a bit after this project by eliminating the witnesses.

My entry into the hospital marked the beginning of a new life for me. Most of the patients were non-Jewish, German political prisoners. The man who performed the surgery on my infected leg was Walter Kramer, the same person who had saved my life earlier. The methods were primitive, and anaesthesia was not available. After the operation, my fate fell into the hands of a Jewish nurse, named Moritz, who was in charge of those who were suffering from frostbite. Moritz was a criminal from Berlin and very tough, a murderer. He wasn't afraid to tangle with the toughest people in the camp.

Life in the hospital was much better than on the outside. An entire barrel of soup was brought in and no one touched it. I was amazed. I had already been reduced to a skeleton. The Germans, as well as those few Jews whose wives were not Jewish, received food packages from home and wouldn't eat the camp food, which was vastly inferior by comparison. It was like being in a sanatorium, or better yet, paradise. I ate as much as I could and came down with a terrible case of diarrhea. But I also gained weight in the hospital and I looked as if I weighed twice as much as when I came in.

Naturally, I racked my brains trying to figure out a way of extending my stay in the hospital. I concluded that if I could make myself indispensable to Moritz, I would be set. I didn't have a lot of competition because most of those in the hospital were politically well-connected Germans who were in no immediate danger of being removed from the hospital. It was Moritz's responsibility to boil hot water on a stove early in the morning. The water was used to heal those whose feet had become frozen from working outside in the cold. The method, known as *wechselbader*, was to first immerse the feet in hot water and then in cold water. Every five minutes he would ring a bell to signal that you had to move your feet from one pot to the other. So I got up early, made the fire and put a large pot of water on it.

When Moritz saw the water boiling, he said: "Who's the *schweinhund* that did this?" And when I admitted it, he hit me, probably because he was afraid that I would take away his job. But I kept on doing it every morning, and every morning he hit me a little less. In fact, I would have done it even if he had severely beaten me up because outside it was cold and snowing, there was very little food, and compared to the rest of Buchenwald, this was heaven. Moritz eventually came to see me as a person who was useful to him, and who could make his job easier.

Moritz was a king in his part of the hospital because, besides caring for the sick, he was in charge of food distribution. In exchange for food, people gave him massages, pedicures, manicures, and fancy clothing smuggled in from outside the camp. He was only a little guy, but he had the power. Every week there was a roll call to inspect the patients' wounds. An SS officer came and the bandages were opened so that he could decide who no longer required treatment and could be released. The examiner wasn't a doctor but the SS also needed jobs to justify its presence in the camp.

Often, it was Moritz who decided who stayed and who had to leave. The SS relied on his judgment when they weren't sure of what to do. Each week Moritz would put salt on my wound the night before so that it would open, look worse, and I would then be able to stay another week. It burned like fire but I was happy to go through it. The man was a criminal, but he saved my life more than once.

All in all, I managed to stay in the hospital for three months. But one day Moritz came in mad like a dog. "Get out, you *schweinhund*, you *dreckische Jude!*" he said. I was shocked at his behavior, especially since he was a Jew himself. I began crying: "Moritz, I did everything you wanted. I worked hard. Why are you throwing me out?" I had grown accustomed to the softer life in the hospital and I was certain that I was no longer capable of living on the outside. Moritz ignored my pleas and I had no choice but to leave. That night the guards came in to the hospital and took all of the sick people to the forest and killed them. Moritz had known about it in advance and chose to save my life.

I returned to the regular camp where I immediately encountered a new problem in the barrack. The *blockaltester*, Martin Gross, had a brother named Willy who was a kapo in the quarry. The two brothers were always fighting with each other. Willy had taken a dislike to me back when I worked in the quarry, for no reason other than the fact that I was an *Ostjüde*. Now he said that I must die for this "offense." He was a Jewish criminal from Berlin and he did his best to have me sent back to the quarry where he would then be able to finish me off.

Fortunately, Martin Gross, although he was also a criminal, protected me. Why? Because I worked hard and was always ready to do whatever was asked of me. Sweep? I swept. Straighten out the room? I straightened. If I saw a button was missing on the *blockaltester's* shirt, I sewed it on. I became like a pet dog to him. That's the only way I can describe it. Because I was obedient, the *blockaltester*, who protected me whenever possible, had me assigned to the Invalid Commando instead of to the quarry, as his brother Willy wanted. This was easy work intended for recuperating inmates. Four people would haul boxes of potato peels or cabbage stalks to the pigs. Whatever the case, this job kept me away from my nemesis, Willy Gross.

One of the major factors that saved my life was my acceptance, in 1942, into the bricklaying school.[2] Applying to it was probably the smartest thing I did while I was in Buchenwald. Most of the other things that happened to me were just luck and not in my control. One of the kapos from Building Commando Two, Robert Siewert, was a longtime Communist party leader. He was an outstanding individual who often saved people from beatings. He had even won a certain grudging admiration for his courage from some of the SS officers. Early on, Siewert suggested to the SS that they create a school for bricklayers. Since Germany needed skilled workers to repair the damage to bombed buildings, the idea met with their approval. Naturally, this was not Siewert's concern; he simply saw it as a way of saving more peoples' lives.

The SS told Siewert to accept only young people between the ages of eighteen and twenty into the detail. There was a place to register, but I didn't even think of going in and trying since I was twenty-six. But then I saw a forty-year-old man come out of the office who told me that he'd been accepted into the school. Hearing this, I discussed it with my best friend Jack Handelsman. He thought it was a good idea and so we both registered and were admitted, receiving an armband with the word "bricklayer" on it.

I first met Handelsman in 1941, when he was given twenty-five lashes for smoking a cigarette in a shack while at work. He was brought to the hospital where Walter Kramer took care of him. Handelsman came from Warsaw, where he had also belonged to Hashomer Hatzair. He was first arrested in October 1940 and sent to Warsaw's Pawiak Prison, an infamous place best known for its torture chambers. From there he was sent to Auschwitz where he helped to build new barracks. After a time he was transferred to the Neuengamme Concentration Camp where he was a laborer. His next stop was Dachau and his job there was to dig up stones.

Finally, in July of 1941, he arrived in Buchenwald and was placed in Block 29, where Erich Eissler, a political prisoner, was the *blokaltester*. He was assigned to the quarry, a terrible place, but standard for newcomers. He became friendly with Elek Greenbaum, the barrack *stubedienst*. Greenbaum took pity on him and helped him transfer into a building commando. Incidentally, Greenbaum had the distinction of having been the first Polish-Jewish *stubedienst*. In the early days, such choice positions were held only by German prisoners.

Handelsman and I decided to register for the bricklaying school because we figured that they couldn't produce bricklayers overnight. Stone carriers yes, but bricklayers no. I also thought that with winter coming it would be better to be indoors in the school. Because we were learning a trade, we were not considered productive like regular workers. Therefore, we received half of the regular rations during our training. But we were willing to eat less in order to be inside, out of the freezing cold. I was also given a pair of old, but real shoes made from leather, in exchange for my wooden clogs, a great improvement. Out of the 400 "students" accepted, about half were Jewish. Why so many Jews? They were overrepresented among the registrants since as Jews they were in the worst commandos and consequently were most likely to improve their situation by becoming bricklayers. Many of the Gentile Poles dropped out because at that time it seemed as if those who volunteered would be very poorly fed. As a result, they concluded that it would be better to work hard in an outdoor commando and get more to eat. But the Jews could not see any better alternatives available, and so they remained.

It turned out to be the best decision of our lives. On October 17, 1942, an order was issued from headquarters in Berlin that all Jewish prisoners in Germany were to be immediately transferred to Auschwitz. At that morning's *appel* (roll call), all of the Jewish bricklayers were ordered to stand off to the side. We were very frightened at being singled out, thinking that they were going to accuse us of sabotage or some other crime, and kill us. Much to our surprise, we were taken away and sent to our new quarters, Block 22.

The rest of the Jews were transported to Auschwitz. Jewish bricklayers were allowed to stay because we were considered workers essential to the war effort. Only about 100 other Jews remained in the camp, primarily German Jews who were old timers and had important positions.

I must say that when we walked into the barrack we became terribly depressed. Everyone knew someone who had gone out on the Auschwitz transport and, as we looked around, the point was driven home that whoever was not there would probably never return. And so it was. Except for a handful of individuals, we never saw them again.

After three months of training we were assigned to the newly formed bricklayer's commando. An additional 500 people were assigned to us as assistants. Their jobs were to dig holes, to carry, to mix cement, and the like, while we did the actual bricklaying. We had an instructor from Berlin and I learned bricklaying, as well as plastering, building arches, and related skills.

Constructing arches was actually quite complicated. It had to be done quickly, while the mortar was still fresh, and it required two people who could work well together. Jack Handelsman was my partner in this and he was, like me, a perfectionist. The other workers, who were more careless in their work, said to us: "Why is it so important that it be perfect? Who are we working for anyway?" Handelsman responded: "I'm not doing it for the Nazis; I'm doing it for myself." The truth was that we became so involved in the job itself that we were able to momentarily forget how small our chances of survival were. Perhaps we wanted to forget.

In 1942, the Germans began constructing the Gustloff Munitions Factory outside of Buchenwald. It was actually a complex of factories. In a relatively short period of time we built an entire town, literally from scratch, with buildings, streets, and sidewalks.

Every morning we were counted and taken outside the camp to work together with German civilians.

Some of the bricklayers were sloppy. They would sometimes spill mortar over the bricks. I never looked up to see if the SS were coming because I was doing my job. But those who weren't good workers ducked under the wall to hide when they saw the SS approaching. As a result, the SS saw only the good workers like me and Handelsman, and when they discovered the spilled mortar or crooked bricks that the others had left, we were blamed and punished with five or ten lashes. But out of a sense of morality, I could never snitch on my fellow inmates and tell who really messed up. The idea of not squealing was also an ironclad rule of the camp Underground.

As time passed, my sense of security increased. As a bricklayer carrying my level and trowel around the camp, I felt less endangered, even by the SS. Even though they could still beat us whenever they felt like it, they had some respect for us as professionals. If we passed an SS officer on the path, we would take off our caps and walk briskly, as if we in a hurry to complete some important task. Most important, once you were in the bricklayers' commando for a while there was only a small chance that you would be removed from it, because we were needed for our skills. We even felt secure enough to do some illegal work. For example, the *blockaltester* would ask us to pour a square block of cement at the front entrance so that inmates wouldn't track mud into the room, without the consent of the SS. Nevertheless, I was always acutely aware that I could be removed from the commando at any time. Nothing was ever certain in Buchenwald.

Notes

1. See Eugen Kogon, *The Theory and Practice of Hell: The German Concentration Camps and the System Behind Them.* New York: Berkley Publishing edition, 1975:103, for a fuller description of this method of torture.
2. Ibid., pp. 170, 185.

The author at age seven, standing by his mother's grave. With him are his father, sisters, and brothers.

Jacob Werber before the war.

After the war.

Jacob Werber and his wife Millie in January, 1946.

The author at Buchenwald on April 9, 1995 at the fiftieth anniversary of his liberation.

The author's daughter Emma at fourteen months, one of the 1,500,000 children who perished in the Holocaust.

Whipping apparatus used at Buchenwald.

Torturing prisoners in Buchenwald by hanging them for hours suspended by their arms and legs. Werber has just been cut down and is lying on the ground.

Children emerging from Buchenwald after liberation, accompanied by Jacob
Werber, far right (top photo), standing behind child.

5

Daily Life in Buchenwald

One day, right after our daily roll call, the barrack head was summoned to the gate to appear before the *rapportführer*. He was told that from now on the Jews would have to sing a new song, every day, on the *appelplatz*, called *"Das Juden Lied"* ("The Song of the Jews"). They had one week in which to learn it. And so it was. No matter how tired we were, no matter how cold or hot the weather, in rain or snow, we had to sing the song. It was a humiliating song that made fun of us and we all hated it, especially the German Jews, who had, at one time, taken great pride in being part of the German nation. In a sense, the German Jews probably found singing this song to be a worse punishment than being beaten. I remember, in particular, the reaction of Professor Heinemann, who considered himself far enough removed from his Jewish ancestors to be an Aryan. When he heard the words of the song, tears rolled down his cheeks. He was in shock. When the time came to actually sing the words, many Jews couldn't bring themselves to do so. They were immediately taken out of the line by the *stubediensts* and beaten into submission. After a while, we got used to the idea, everyone sang it, and the words became something of a bitter joke to us:

Das Juden Lied

For hundreds of years we cheated the nation.
No swindle was too great for us.
We manipulated, lied, and cheated
with either kronen or marks.

We are the Cohens, the Isaacs, and the Wolfensteiners.
We are known by our animal faces.
If there is a race worse than we are,
then it must be related to us.
Now our Paradise has come to an end.
Gone is our filth and our tricks.
Now our idle hands
Will have to perform real labor.

Now the Germans have seen through us
And have put us securely behind barbed wire.
We, the cheaters of the nation, always feared this possibility,
Which has happened so suddenly, overnight it seems.

Now our crooked Jewish noses are in mourning.
For in vain are our efforts to plant seeds of hatred.
Now there will be no more stealing, carousing, and high living.
It is too late now, forever too late.

The most famous of the songs we sang at the *appelplatz* was
"The Buchenwald Song." Forcing the prisoners, regardless of nationality, to sing it after evening roll call, was the brainchild of
Senior Camp Officer Rodl. In part it was an attempt to fool visitors as to the true nature of camp life. Since the Nazis insisted on
perfection, it was often necessary to start the song five or ten times,
before it was rendered in a satisfactory manner. As for the singers,
they soon grew to hate it and the more daring among them would
silently mouth the words. The Buchenwald Song was written by
an Austrian Jew, and it was rumored that he was murdered for it. A
few months later, his sin was forgotten, and they made us sing it!
When we ended the song, we sang "to be free" so loud it echoed
through the woods. For us, this was a form of defying the Nazis'
authority, as well as giving us hope:

Das Buchenwald Lied

At the break of day,
When the sun laughs,
The columns make their way,
To perform the daily chores,
In the grey light of morning.

And the forest is black
And the sky red,
And in our bag we carry a piece of bread.
And in our hearts, in our hearts, we carry our sorrows.

Oh, Buchenwald, I can never forget you,
Because this is my fate.
But when I shall leave you, I will truly appreciate
How wonderful it is to be free.
Yet Buchenwald, we neither cry nor complain,
No matter what our fate may be,
We will nevertheless, say yes to life
For soon will come the day, when we shall be free.

And the blood is hot,
And my sweetheart is far away.
And the wind blows softly.
And my love for you is so great
When you remain true to me; yes, stay true to me!
And the rocks are hard, but our steps are steady.
And we carry our picks and spades,
And in our hearts, our hearts, our love.

Oh, Buchenwald...

Though the night is short
And the day so long—
This song sounds
Like the songs of our Fatherland.
We do not allow our courage to be robbed from us.
Stay fast to your path and do not lose your courage.
For we carry our will to live in our blood
And in our hearts, our hearts our faith.
Oh Buchenwald...

One popular underground song, "The Peat-Bog Soldiers," was
often sung at work. Its words had special meaning for us:

The Peat-Bog Soldiers

Far and wide as the eye can wander
Heath and bog are everywhere.
Not a bird sings out to cheer us,
Oaks are standing gaunt and bare.

We are the peat-bog soldiers
We're marching with our spades to the bog.

Up and down the guards are pacing,
No one, no one can go through.
Fight would mean a sure death.
Guns and barbed wire greet our view.

We are the peat-bog soldiers...

But for us there is no complaining,
Winter will in time be past.
One day we shall cry rejoicing,
Homeland dear, you're mine at last.

Then will the peat-bog soldiers
March no more with spades to the bog.

There was a certain permanent state of tension that came from the need to constantly be on one's guard. Whenever the foremen, or kapos, yelled "Eighteen!," it meant the Nazis were coming. We also had to constantly watch out when other prisoners whom we didn't know, approached the barrack, since they might be collaborators.

People were very touchy with each other. If you would brush up against someone, they could become very angry. Mistakes at roll call were very common and when they occurred we would have to stand on the *appelplatz* for hours until they corrected them. One day, a pig was found missing from the pigsty. They took away our food and water for three days, saying: "The Jews stole the pig." Of course, we hadn't done it. We wouldn't have dared.

One of the most frightening things about camp life was its unpredictability. The atmosphere could change dramatically from day to day, even from half hour to half hour. For example, a newly arrived Nazi commandant heard of a rumor spread by the prisoners that he was a decent human being. In response, he made an announcement over the camp microphone: "I heard that you think I'm a nice guy. Well, I'll show you how nice I am!" He proceeded to make our life hell for weeks. We had to do everything on the run for almost a month and often with loads on our back. Hundreds collapsed from exhaustion.

If an officer passed by and you didn't take off your cap, it was a big crime and you could get twenty-five lashes with either a whip or a cane. The whole camp would be made to watch.[1] The inmate was strapped on his stomach with his legs pushed forward and his head down on a rack made from wood so that his backside was fully exposed. It wasn't customary to give more than 25 lashes, but on occasion they gave more, sometimes as much as double that amount. They used different types of whips made from leather, wood, or steel. They didn't respect us for enduring pain because we weren't worth respecting. To the Nazis we were simply not human.

I remember how in May of 1941, a Jew named Hempel, was thrown into a hole filled with water by *Hauptsturmführer* Abraham. He tried to get out but Abraham pushed him back in with his boot and he drowned. To mock the prisoners, the SS conducted a phony investigation into the cause of his death. The entire commando of thirty-four Jews, including his brother, testified as to what happened. After they had finished the Nazis arrested them and murdered them at the rate of three or four people a day, until all who had testified were dead.

Our captors were fanatical about doing everything in a particular proper manner. For example, they could kill a person but they would never hit someone with their glasses on. They would say "Take off your glasses," and then they would beat you. This was because their rule was that you couldn't hit a person while he was wearing his glasses. Perhaps they were afraid of getting their hands cut.

The Nazis took particular delight in torturing us on our Jewish holidays. For instance, on Purim, in 1941, they took out ten young Jewish boys, the strongest ones, and they killed them off. "This is for Haman," they said.

In the camp a group of Jews got together to pray.[2] One of the prisoners, Gustav Schiller, a deputy *blockaltester*, mocked them, saying: "To whom are you praying? Where is God now that we need him? If there is a God, let him kill me now." I told him many times not to make fun of the religious inmates, to let them pray if they believed in it. Maybe their belief would give them the strength to survive. But this did not have much of an effect on him. Realizing that I had to be more firm, I told him one day: "Look, you have to stop bothering the religious prisoners or you're going to be in serious trouble." He stared hard into my eyes and realized that I meant business. He became frightened that the Underground would have him lose his position and privileges, and would send him to the quarry. From that day on he never bothered them again. Schiller was from Lvov, Poland, but he spoke German fluently and he looked like an Aryan. I'm not even sure that "Schiller" was his real name.

Looking back, it's understandable why Schiller was cynical about religion. Others, myself included, asked, "How can one believe in God after all this?" It was not an easy question. The Germans slaughtered children, religious Jews, yeshiva students and rabbis as easily as they killed nonreligious Jews and sinners. Where was God then? Each year we retold the stories of how God performed miracles to save His chosen people. We remembered the Passover miracles: the Jews being freed from Egypt, and the parting of the Red Sea. We read the Book of Esther, and how the Jews were miraculously spared from death at the hand of their enemies. Well, we had no Moses in the camps. We had no Queen Esther. Why had God forgotten His people in this time of our greatest need? If it was God's plan to punish us, what had we done? And if perhaps we adults had been so wicked that we deserved such devastation, what had all of the murdered children done? The majority of Polish Jews were God-fearing and observant and yet most were killed. I, on the other hand, was spared by what seemed to be chance. Why?

It seemed that every day we faced a new problem. One day we were accused of sabotage, another day someone was caught without a shirt or with a missing button—five lashes. You could even be punished for putting your hands in your pockets to protect yourself from the cold. One day they would decide that we walked too slowly and would punish us by making the prisoners go everywhere on the run. If someone was missing we had to stay at the *appelplatz* until he was found—dead or alive. And we would have to stand there singing the "Buchenwald Song" and the "Song of the Jews" over and over again past the point where our voices became hoarse. The soup was usually brought to the barracks at 5:00 P.M. but if we were delayed, perhaps even beaten up, until 10:00 P.M., then by the time we got there the soup would be cold. But who cared about subhumans? Certainly not our captors.

Even the littlest things were fraught with peril. Take for example the "toilet" facilities when we were in the tents, before being transferred to the permanent camp. We had to stand on a wooden board to relieve ourselves, over a hole dug out of the ground. If two people were not careful and stood on one side of the plank, it would tip over, and both of them would fall into the pile of feces.

While the beatings were terrible, and the hunger unbearable, we knew that things could be much worse. We heard horrible stories about the medical experiments performed on prisoners in Block 46—people purposely exposed to typhus or put naked into ice water. In fact, I was offered double rations to try a "new medicine." Even though I was very thin and starving, I didn't volunteer because my *blockaltester* advised against it. Such things were always dangerous because the Nazis never would allow witnesses to survive who could later tell what the Germans had done.

One of the reasons I survived is probably because I was very observant. I watched everything around me. I tried to follow orders and not stick out too much. Also, I could adjust very easily. I learned quickly what needed to be done in each new situation. Since I had no hope that I would ever be free, I said to myself: "I'm a slave; I was born a slave." It's hard to explain it. I don't know. But above all else, it was luck, or coincidence. I did very few things on purpose to survive.

Once, when I was in the Invalid Commando, they called people for a transport and I was once again lucky that I didn't go. The SS had criminals who were their spies. These collaborators spread a rumor that the Red Cross from Switzerland had taken over Dachau and had made it into a camp for invalids and the sick. Furthermore, according to the rumor, we wouldn't have to work and there were libraries, movie theaters, and good food in Dachau. We also heard that, after the war, the Germans would exchange the inmates there for their own prisoners of war. So everybody was jealous of me because, as a worker in the Invalid Commando, it seemed that I had already "made it." Well, I showed up for the selection on the *appelplatz*. It was winter and very cold, but they made us strip anyway. It always seemed like they made us undress in the wintertime and never when the weather was nice and warm.

But my effort was unsuccessful. They kicked me out of the group, even knocked out two of my teeth in the process. "What are you doing here?," they yelled. In fact, I was only there because I had, through my connections, been put into the Invalid Commando. But I looked very healthy compared to the rest of them, and therefore unacceptable for this transport. So I thought, maybe I'll ask Moritz to let me into the hospital for a day so I could be considered sick and allowed to go to Dachau. But Moritz said to me: "Listen, you crazy dog; never swim against the stream. If they didn't take you, don't try to go." And what happened to those selected for the transport to Dachau? They were all taken to the forest and killed. The authorities then sent letters to their relatives saying: "They died."

The fact is you can't really tell how a person will do under these circumstances. I knew wonderful people who became beasts. In the beginning people didn't steal but later on quite a few people stopped caring about how they behaved. New arrivals who came in 1944 included people from other camps who hadn't learned the way things were done in Buchenwald. In essence, the camp brought out both the best and the worst in people because it was a place where no one had any titles or degrees. You were just whomever you were and so the real person emerged, good and bad.

Jewish intellectuals had a particular problem in the camp. This was because in Europe they were a separate class of people who didn't associate much with the rest of the Jews. Their heads were in the clouds, dealing with lofty philosophical issues, without having a good sense of what real life was about. They were different than the politicals, because while the politicals often dealt with the same issues, they were by and large from the working class, and knew quite well the meaning of struggling for a living. In Europe when Jewish intellectuals achieved a higher status than the average Jew, they became less involved in the community and some even left it entirely. Very seldom would you encounter a religious doctor or a religious lawyer. The intellectuals often thought they were better than everyone and so they couldn't handle being treated like everyone else in the camp. Furthermore, the Nazis were tougher on them as well and gave them hell. They said: "A doctor? Go to work and see what work is." Maybe they did it out of sadism or maybe because if a Jew was less than human, as they believed, then what was he doing as a doctor?[3]

All I can say is that you could generally expect more from a simple person than from the intelligentsia. And if an intellectual got real power, as a *blockaltester* or a kapo, they behaved the worst. Often an ordinary person like a truck driver or a common laborer had the courage to do things that were very risky in order to help others. As simple people they knew what suffering was. This is a fact.

Physical strength was not necessarily the key to survival. I knew quite a few men who possessed enormous strength who perished nonetheless. One example was Henoch Raichman, who was a barrack mate of mine in 1942. A truck driver, he came from Warsaw and was a very strong man, a giant. He was also strong-willed and often refused to obey orders from the kapos, for which he was usually beaten. I felt sorry for him and told him not to resist, that he couldn't win. In fact, I patched things up between him and the kapos and he never forgot it until his last day.

Later on, when I was a *trager*, a carrier, in the Building Commando, Henoch said he would be my partner. He wanted to show his appreciation by helping me out. Because he was so strong, he thought that if he were my partner he could ease my burden. His large build eventually was his undoing. Due to his size, he suffered terribly from hunger. He'd eat garbage, spoiled food, and as a result he became seriously ill. He sank lower and lower, losing a great deal of weight until finally he looked like a skeleton, what we called a *musulman*. By then I was stronger than him, but he remained in the forefront. At one point, after a particularly brutal beating, he collapsed and died. His last words were: "I can't anymore."

Food was perhaps our most obsessive concern. We thought about it day and night. We were constantly talking about the delicious food that we had eaten at home, how on Friday night we had challah, gefilte fish, chicken, and *tzimmes*. We even exchanged recipes for chulent, potato kugel, whatever. Some walked away from these conversations, complaining that it made them even hungrier; but for others, it was a way of going on.

Every morning we were given some heavy black bread, about 200 grams. I always saved my bread. On occasion, I exchanged my margarine for spoiled red beets, which I ate. I did this because I knew that the beets would cause me to feel sick and lose my appetite. In this way I was able to save my bread for a few days until my stomach got better. Then I would eat the bread that had accumulated and I would have a feast. On Wednesday they would give out oatmeal and this is what I dreamed about the whole week—the oatmeal.

It was in Buchenwald that I learned the meaning of bread. How easy it is for us to take it for granted! We do so today, and we did so in my earlier life in Radom. In Buchenwald, a slice of bread could measure the value of a life. What would one do to get another piece of bread with which to sustain another hour or another day of life? Reader, what would you do for a piece of bread? Betray your friend? Take bread out of the hand of someone who was dying anyway? Steal it from the inmate next to you, when he was not looking? Kill for it? Or would you hold on to your values in the face of the strongest of temptations, ever present, gnawing hunger? Once you received a piece of bread, would you wolf it down, hoard it, or share it? You can speculate how you would have behaved in Buchenwald, but you can never know for sure unless you were actually there.

In truth, it is impossible to describe what hunger in a concentration camp was really like, to those who have not been there, what an extra bite of bread meant. The inmates were so desperate that they were willing to risk twenty-five lashes just for the opportunity to grab a rotten potato or turnip. When a person ate his small piece of bread, he would almost always put one hand under the other so as not to lose even a crumb.

I remember how one time in the Small Camp a son was lying next to his father and the son died. The father did not report the death and when they came to give out the bread, he raised the dead son's hand in order to obtain his son's portion. But when the other people saw this they began screaming until the body was removed.

People rarely stole bread because if they were caught they were usually sent to the quarry which meant almost certain death. Eventually Handelsman was appointed as our barrack's *stubedienst*, and was in charge of distributing the rations. He was very fair and always weighed the bread to insure that everyone received the same amount. He was so scrupulously careful. He even devised a crude scale for this purpose. He weighed the bread as if it were precious gold. Whenever he saw one piece of bread that weighed more than another he would cut off the extra amount and attach it with a splinter of wood, the size of a toothpick, to a second piece that weighed a little less. In this way the amounts given out were equalized.

But not everyone was like that. There was a man in Buchenwald with a reputation for having been an honest person in a previous camp. As a result, he was appointed to the position of *tischalteste* for the childrens' table. Imagine our surprise when he was caught stealing the pieces of attached bread for himself. As a punishment, the *blockaltester* put a brick in each of his hands and forced him to stand there holding his hands up with a sign that said: "I stole bread from children." The man went downhill very quickly after that out of shame for what he had done and he died soon after this incident.

One of my fellow inmates was a *landsman* from Radom whom I had known as a youth. On one occasion, he was caught stealing a portion of bread. Of course this was wrong, but I protected him. I saved his life but I warned him not to do it again. Then he stole again, and I told him: "If you steal once more I won't be able to save you." But it didn't happen again. And I should add that we made sure that the victim of this theft was given another portion equivalent to what had been stolen from him. Today this man, who under such dire circumstances gave in to temptation and stole the bread, lives in the U.S. Whenever we meet, he tells everyone around that I am the man who saved his life, sparing the details of how this happened.

When I was in the Invalid Commando, part of my job was to take the potato peels and cabbage stalks from the kitchen to the pigsty. I tied a rope around the bottoms of my pants, where the cuffs would normally be, so that when I would stick the "food" inside the top, it would fall to the bottom and be trapped there. Later, after I returned to the barrack, I removed whatever edible scraps I had hidden in my pants. My friends then cooked a soup out of these items, which we all shared. Indeed, we made all kinds of dishes, which under these conditions we considered delicacies, although you wouldn't see them on the menu in the Waldorf-Astoria. Because I could get this "food" I was considered a philanthropist by my fellow inmates. It was risky but even though death might be the punishment for stealing a potato, you did it anyway, because food was everything and our attitude towards life was very different.

Hans Reiner, one of the *blockaltester's* deputies, once came across a rare find, a dead cat. It had probably been electrocuted on the wires. He skinned it and my friend, Handelsman, cooked it. Handelsman gave me a piece to eat. Nothing ever tasted so delicious to a starving man. It was the most memorable culinary experience of my five and a half years in Buchenwald.

There was a "bank" in camp and when someone came in with money they had to deposit it into their account. Officially, prisoners could draw only thirty marks a month in Buchenwald camp scrip from their accounts, but the Jews were often unable to gain access to their funds at all. The Nazis would accuse them falsely of, say, stealing a pig, dirtying a wall, or other "crimes" and then, as punishment, they would refuse to give them their monthly amount. I, personally, didn't have this problem because I came to the camp without any money.

The money couldn't really be used for much in the camp since mostly we just bartered items—bread for margarine, cigarettes, or some similar exchange. It was, however, accepted at the camp canteen, which was open from time to time. The canteen sold things like moldy dog biscuits or spoiled food. Once in a while cigarettes would be available. The items varied according to whatever had come in that month.

Sunday was officially considered the day of rest, but this did not necessarily apply to Jews. There was, for instance, the Landscaping Commando. Those assigned to it didn't really do gardening or lawn mowing. Most of the work was in wooded areas. Its main job consisted of pulling out roots and tree stumps. All of us tried to avoid it like the plague but once you were chosen for it, there was no alternative. We were hit with clubs and sticks and chased out of the barracks. It was a terrible commando because the officer in charge, Lieutenant Dumbock, was an animal who enjoyed beating and killing people. If you fell he would step on your throat until you died. He never went home without having killed a few people during the day. Those unlucky enough to be in this commando during the week were truly cursed and we frequently heard reports of such unfortunates committing suicide.

On Sundays Dumbock would round up any unfortunate Jews he could find, and make them do a shift in the Landscaping Commando. There were many times when I returned from "landscaping" with a bloody lip or bruises, but one thing we knew—if you fell you had to get up right away or you were dead.

In 1944, the bricklayers were ordered to build a new building in camp, the purpose of which was unclear. We had already learned about the gas chambers, and we speculated that they were probably building one in Buchenwald. In turned out that we built a whorehouse for the Aryan prisoners at Buchenwald. Perhaps the

Nazis thought they could rely on their countrymen, or perhaps they might some day come back into power and so it was worthwhile providing them with "recreational" activities. The twenty or so women were sent there from Ravensbruck Concentration Camp. The women were treated like pets by the SS men. Each day they would take them out for walks. After a month or so the women were completely worn out. They would be killed and replaced by a fresh contingent of women from Ravensbruck. The political prisoners, because they didn't want to exploit other prisoners, and the Jehovah's Witnesses, for religious reasons, refused to participate in yet another example of barbarity.

The camp had a library, but who had the time, or the inclination, to read books in such an atmosphere? There was also a movie theater in Buchenwald, the only one in any concentration camp, as far as I know. Once in a while, we were brought there and shown newsreels about how the Germans were winning the war. On those occasions we had to be very careful. There was always the possibility of being accused of being a homosexual if you accidentally touched the person next to you on the bench or if you sat too close to him for warmth, because, during the winter, we were always freezing in our thin clothes. The Nazis knew that this was rarely the case but it was entertainment for them to attack us in this way.

Notes

1. For more on these public punishments, see Walter Poller, *Butchers of Buchenwald.* New York: Zebra Books paperback edition, 1977:126–132.
2. Pierre D'Harcourt, author of *The Real Enemy.* New York: Scribner's, 1967, was a Frenchman who came to the camp in 1943. He notes that there were Orthodox Jews from Poland and Romania in the camp who met to pray "in small, secret whispering groups between the huts." p. 136.
3. Eugen Kogon, citing the case of the French deportees who arrived at Buchenwald in 1943, also notes that intellectuals had special problems in adapting to camp life. *The Theory and Practice of Hell*, p. 196.

6

I Join the Underground

In 1942, I was approached by Emil Carlebach to join the Buchenwald International Underground. He was a German-Jewish communist who was also my *blockaltester* in Barrack 22. Carlebach was a teenager when he was first arrested as a political enemy after Hitler came to power in 1933. His parents were able to secure his release and sent him to England. But he returned to Germany to fight Nazism and was arrested again. He had spent time in many prisons before being sent to newly established Buchenwald in 1937, where he helped build the camp. Carlebach survived the war and now lives in Frankfurt. After all these years, he remains faithful to the ideals of his youth.

The other powerful force in the camp was the criminal group which was the sworn enemy of the Underground. The criminals had initially been put into power by the SS, which felt that they could be relied upon to control and brutalize the inmates. They had come to Buchenwald about the same time as the politicals, in 1937. Brought in from Sachsenhausen and various prisons, both groups had built the camp, so each was pretty well entrenched from the start.

Eventually, the Underground was able to take control of the camp from the criminal element, but not before hundreds lost their lives as a result of the struggle. Gradually, the Underground succeeded in putting its own people into leadership positions, as *stubediensts* and *blockalteste*. The criminals' ranks were thinned out over time by removing them from key positions for various infractions.

73

Morally, the Nazis were on the same level as the criminals and liked them because they were willing collaborators. However, if they caught the criminals stealing from the other inmates, they took action against them. The punishment was usually a transfer to the quarry. Those few who remained saw what was happening and changed their behavior.

The Underground was originally organized by, and made up almost entirely of German communists and social democrats, including German Jews. At first, the Underground was a very small group, but it gradually grew by taking in different types of members. There were German Jehovah's Witnesses, imprisoned for being conscientious objectors, who were members. The Jehovah's Witnesses were highly principled individuals. Later on, the Underground accepted people from other nationalities, and eventually they admitted non-German Jews.

Carlebach approached me while I was still in the Invalid Commando. I suspect that he saw me as an underprivileged person who had nothing to lose and who would benefit most from true order and justice in the camp. In short, the perfect recruit. Also, since I always assumed the demeanor of a simple drone, the Underground's enemies wouldn't suspect that I had the brains or initiative to notice their crimes or hurt them. Finally, the Underground's policies toward admitting nonpoliticals into their ranks had changed. In the struggle with the criminals over control of the camp, a number of non-political prisoners had shown great courage and had strongly supported the political group. Therefore, they were finally willing to allow outsiders like me into their ranks. Carlebach said to me:

"You see how they're constantly beating up the people. You see how they steal the food from you. Would you like things to be better run?" And I said:

"Sure, I would."

"So would you like to join the organization?" he asked.

"Yes," I responded.

"But do you know, that when they hung those people two weeks ago, those were our people?"

"Yes, I know," I answered, "but I have nothing to lose."

One day, Ilse Koch passed by the building we were putting up and noticed a bare-chested man, a German prisoner named Hans, who was working with me on the scaffold. She became intrigued by his tattoos and wrote down his number. That evening, at the *appel*, his number was called and he was told to come to the gate. There, he was taken away and executed. His skin was removed and brought to the tannery to be made into parchment for a lampshade. The Jehovah's Witnesses were the only ones who worked there and they refused to do this. So the Nazis hanged three of them, one after the other, to scare the others into obeying but it didn't help and they gave up in their efforts.[1] Instead, the skin was taken to Weimar to be made up.

The Jehovah's Witnesses were the most compassionate people—they gave their own bread away to those more hungry than them. They were saints who were staunchly against the evils of Hitler. They spoke openly and proudly about their religion but they didn't try to convert anyone.

My thinking had to do with my life before the war when I was a leader in Hashomer Hatzair. I was an idealist. I had wanted to work on a kibbutz, to help build up a country that would be a normal nation like all others. So it was not surprising that I now wanted to be part of a progressive political movement within Buchenwald. In addition, the socialist ideals of the Underground's members, while non-Zionist, were very similar to Hashomer Hatzair's general outlook. The risks of getting involved didn't really enter my mind because I didn't think I would ever come out alive anyway.

The Underground identified us, not as Jews, but according to the country we came from, whether it was Poland, or Hungary, or elsewhere. Only the Nazis saw us as Jews first. Thus, the German Jews and non-Jews were seen as having a common background and were grouped together. Their thinking was similar, although this was not necessarily the case for other groups, for example, the Poles and the Polish Jews.

Credit must be given to the German communists and social democrats whose strong will and ideological commitment made the Underground a success. I should add that even among the presumably idealistic and selfless politicals not everyone was a saint.[2] They were, however, highly disciplined so that even those who weren't good people had to behave themselves. The communists did exhibit some favoritism. They were much slower to take action against bad communists than against wrongdoers in general.

The German inmates respected the German Jews much more than the *Ostjuden,* because they had things in common. They spoke the same language, had similar education and cultural background and they sometimes even came from the same town. A good number of the German Jews looked down on us too, especially if they were educated. When they heard us speaking Yiddish they would say in a derogatory manner: "Stop Yeedling." In later years, the German prisoners became the minority as more and more Eastern Europeans were sent to Buchenwald.

The network of contacts within the Underground was arranged so that each person knew only those whom he had to know. In this way, there was less of a chance of someone being betrayed. Even today, I can find people who were with me in Buchenwald but were unaware that I was in the Underground. Conversely, I'm sure there were other inmates whose Underground affiliations I didn't know about. All in all, I would say there were probably only about ten Polish Jews in the Underground. Besides me, there was Jack Handelsman, Israel Frankel, Gustav Schiller, Baruch Goldberg, Eliyahu "Elek" Greenbaum, and several others. I served as the group's contact person to the general Underground. Only after the war, through published accounts, did we learn more about the general leaders. After all, no one was formally registered. Sometimes, when circumstances called for it, the Polish Jewish cell met as a group, but generally we avoided this since we did not want to call attention to ourselves.

My involvement with the Underground grew over a period of time. For example, I was asked to find out if the *blockaltester* was justified in beating someone up. On other occasions, I reported to Carlebach which kapos were treating the prisoners harshly. He would ask another Underground member to take them aside and warn them in the strongest possible terms to stop acting this way. When one of our members approached the Nazis about this matter, he tried to appeal to their self-interest. He pointed out that beating prisoners would not increase production one iota. Quite a few kapos were decent people and beat the prisoners superficially when they were accused of breaking the rules. The purpose of this was to save them from far worse beatings at the hands of the Nazis. On the other hand, there were also kapos who so closely identified with our mutual persecutors that they took their responsibilities too seriously, above and beyond what was actually required of them.

Food was everything in Buchenwald, and thus it was also a potential source of conflict, greed, and corruption. There were *blockalteste* and *stubediensts* who took advantage of their positions to steal highly prized foods from prisoners who received packages from the outside, or worse yet, stole food entrusted to them by the SS for distribution to the inmates in their barracks. They would brazenly steal whole loaves and sell them for camp scrip. An example of another food worthwhile for them to steal was a cheap type of cold cut, called *blutwurst,* which we occasionally received. We would each get only a small piece, about a quarter of an inch thick, but for us it was a great delicacy. Stealing the inmates' rations was the most immoral of acts, for in doing so, these *blockalteste* and *stubediensts* were not stealing from the SS, they were stealing food out of the mouths of starving inmates. It's important to understand that those who engaged in these acts were simply amoral criminals.

Generally, the stolen items were sold outside the camp by workers fortunate to have assignments in factories or other locations outside of Buchenwald. With the proceeds they bought from outside contacts chocolate, candy, silk scarves, shaving cream, and other goods on behalf of the corrupt *blockalteste* and *stubediensts.*

With these goods, they were able to further enhance their life-style and gain greater power. It was a moral obligation for me to let the Underground know if a *blockaltester* or *stubedienst* were stealing, and if so, where they were hiding stolen salamis, cheeses, and other items.

Usually, I reported to my contact after the evening *appel*. One Wednesday, for example, I reported to the Underground that I saw two salamis hanging behind the closet that were supposed to have been served on Monday. When they heard this, the Underground leadership reported the *blockaltester* and a few of his helpers to the SS, who then assigned them to the quarry. The SS was angry about these thefts because whatever meager portions they provided were Reich property, and should go where they were intended. At this point I was the eyes and ears of the Underground.

There were many non-Jewish prisoners who worked in facto-ries outside of the camp and had access to the better, non-camp food. When they would return to camp in the evening they didn't need the camp food because they'd already eaten outside. The Underground forced those who didn't voluntarily give their extra camp food to others, to do so. Then there was food that came from packages sent from outside. If, for example, an inmate had a wife or other family member on the outside, he could then receive food packages from them. So he had extra. Included in this category were Jews who had non-Jewish wives.

Try to imagine the scene. At one table perhaps fifteen living skel-etons are having a "meal" consisting of a small piece of bread and watered-down soup. The other six sitting there have before them what appears to be the remainder a feast—a piece of cheese or maybe even a sausage from the outside. They hold tightly onto the last scraps of their bounty and refuse to share any with their comrades.

To compel cooperation from those who had more than enough food but refused to share, the Underground leaders would punish them for minor infractions, things that they might normally have overlooked. They would say things like: "Your utensils are dirty, or your bed isn't made properly." They had the power and were willing to use it to demonstrate that those who were selfish had to share with those less fortunate.

Our leaders pointed out to the SS that if the food sent to the prisoners was not eaten within twenty-four hours it would attract roaches. As a result, the SS made it a rule that the food had to be eaten within one day. This prevented hoarding and, in effect, forced the prisoners to share with others that which they couldn't eat right away.

Acceptance into the Underground was certainly a factor in my survival. Their people were in key positions and, in many ways, really ran the camp, even though it was the Nazis who supervised them. The Underground made sure that the ill and elderly political prisoners and the old-timers, were put on the good details such as darning socks or working in the mailroom. They sent collaborators to the quarry or to slave on the railway lines.

The members of the Underground carried out a wide range of activities. Kapos who were too eager to beat prisoners for no reason, mysteriously disappeared after interrogations by Underground leaders. These leaders also arranged for extra food to be given to children who were, even as early as 1941, sheltered in various barracks run by cooperative *blockalteste*. Still others made mittens out of blanket fragments for those who worked in difficult outdoor commandos under conditions of freezing cold.

From 1942 on, the prisoners had their own police force that enforced internal discipline, guarded food and supplies, and which welcomed new arrivals. The idea for this was proposed by Underground members who had the ear of the SS. They explained that these policemen would help to keep order in the camp and make it easier for the Germans to administrate Buchenwald. The Underground saw the creation of such a police force as an opportunity to prepare and train people to actively resist the Nazis. The police even had special blue uniforms, black berets and shiny boots. Their armbands identified them as "*Lagerschutz*," or "Camp Police." The SS tried to get the Camp Police to serve as informers or to perform other dirty deeds for them. These attempts usually failed because the Camp Police were largely under the control of the political prisoners. The Jehovah's Witnesses, however, refused to join the Camp Police, due to their pacifist beliefs.

In 1944, when the number of transports coming from the liquidated ghettoes increased, a new Small Camp was established to warehouse the multitude awaiting their fate—to be shipped either to satellite work camps or to death camps. I was sent to the Small Camp to investigate and report on conditions there. It was a miserable hellhole. People fought like wild dogs over the food and, as opposed to the permanent camp, there was no one to control the situation. After my report about these conditions in the Small Camp they removed the *blockaltester* and the *stubedienst* and replaced them with others.

A lot of survivors who say they were in Buchenwald were actually only "tourists" there. They generally came late, in 1944, when conditions were much better than in the earlier years. By then, the Underground had gained firmer control of the camp and people were treated more humanely. In any event, for most of them, Buchenwald was a temporary stop on the way to either death or labor camps. Many went to Slieben and Dora, where they were usually worked to death. I had a cousin, Manes, who came in 1944. I brought him bread and soup and warned him not to volunteer for any transports unless he checked with me first. But he didn't listen and he volunteered to work in Camp Slieben. Weeks later I saw him in the camp hospital, after he had come back from Slieben, half-dead.

"Why did you do it? I told you not to."

"Yeah," he answered, "I was afraid that if I remained in the Small Camp, and wasn't sent out to work, that I would be identified as a useless person and killed. So, when some of my friends said that we'd get good food in Slieben and that the work would be pretty easy, I went." A few days later he died.

The Underground decided that each newly arrived nationality should be in charge of its own—Belgians, French, Poles, whatever. Their experience in other camps had been that whenever one group dominated, other groups didn't receive justice. A central committee was formed with representatives from each group. Of course, the SS knew nothing about this committee.

In the summer of 1944, Carlebach told us about a transport of several thousand Jews that was coming in from Skarzysko, a town not too far from Radom. At Skarzysko there was a large ammunition factory which employed many Jews as slave labor. As the Red Army approached Skarzysko, the slave labor camp was liquidated and the inmates were dispersed, the bulk of whom were transported to Buchenwald. Handelsman, Gustav Schiller, and I, greeted them upon their arrival. I made a speech to them in Yiddish in which I emphasized that here there were no gas chambers and that the showers had real water. It was important to say this because the new arrivals were afraid to enter the showers, thinking they would be gassed. They remained skeptical even after I spoke, so we told them not to fear; that we would accompany them into the showers. They were surprised at the whole situation—clean clothes, food, Jewish inmates walking around and talking to them. This was very different from where they had been before.[3] Gustav spoke with them about collaborators, saying: "If there are among you people who collaborated with the Germans, report them to us now and we will take care of them." At that time no one stepped forward because they were still afraid. It took weeks and weeks before they had enough confidence to tell us and then, little by little, we learned the identities of these collaborators.

We also explained to them that money had no real value here, namely, that you couldn't bribe people. One Jew who knew me from Kozienice, a redhaired fellow named Leibel, shoved a folded $20.00 U.S. bill into my hand. It was a clearly a bribe, given in the hopes of getting better treatment. I took a match and burned it in front of all these new arrivals. In this way they learned that at this time there was strong and organized opposition to bribery and corruption in Buchenwald and that you couldn't better your conditions here with money. Many of the newcomers had come from ghettos and camps where moral inhibitions had broken down. Generally, in such places, people only helped those who were their close friends or relatives, or who offered them diamonds and money. Until now many of these newcomers had been able to survive only through bribery. Although an important lesson was taught by burning the money, it may have been put to better use when the war was ending, and currency was sorely needed to buy ammunition and guns and to bribe SS men.

On the surface I was just a *stubedienst*, a caretaker, in Block 23, but some of the people suspected that I was also a member of the Underground despite my denials. They knew that if they wanted something done they could come to me. Eventually, however, the Underground arranged for me to be given a formal position—secretary in charge of checking in new arrivals. The newcomers had swelled Buchenwald's population to 85,000. Accordingly, the Underground needed new recruits. I, along with several other old-timers, assumed the responsibility of deciding who should be allowed into the organization. This involved looking into the backgrounds of people, and learning about what they were like prior to their arrival in Buchenwald. Our aim was to separate the collaborators from those who did not betray their fellow human beings.

We were painfully aware that we couldn't possibly help more than a small portion of the camp population, perhaps hundreds out of many thousands.[4] And so we were selective, focusing on certain leaders, people who had excellent general reputations and fathers with children. My overall approach was to help, whenever possible, those whose situation was most desperate.

There were times when we made mistakes in judgment, choosing recruits for the movement who were not so great. For example, I helped a friend from school and then, after the war, I found out that he was a collaborator with many dead Jews on his conscience.

While we tried to exclude the collaborators, there were problems. Those who came in with the collaborators were afraid to report them at first because they feared that the collaborators might get jobs at Buchenwald despite such efforts and exact revenge. To conduct our investigations we would send in our own people to find out what was going on. To blend in, they removed their striped uniforms and put on old and ragged clothing similar to that worn by those in the Small Camp.

The greatest challenge was to conduct a thorough and fair investigation because verifying claims and accusations under these circumstances was often difficult. We were, after all, in a concentration camp and we couldn't send private investigators to, say, a person's home community to check out the stories we heard. But we didn't just take someone's accusations at face value. The Underground investigated all charges. There had to be witnesses, and quite a few, not just one or two people, to make the charges stand up. The accused collaborators were judged in a formal court proceeding. We made sure that the judge was of the same nationality so that he could understand their language well. More important, if we did this, the defendant wouldn't be able to claim that the judge, say a Hungarian or a Czech, was prejudiced against him because he was a Pole or a Russian.

We were so careful that even after we reached a decision we waited a few days before carrying it out so that anyone with new evidence could come forward. Sometimes though, it wasn't possible to have a trial because the anger of the inmates was so great that they gave the collaborator their own brand of justice, killing him right away, without waiting for a trial.

The new arrivals came from ghettos and camps where there was no justice and no pity. So when they saw that we distributed bread and water to the new arrivals almost immediately, they realized things were different here and they were quite surprised. We told the people that if someone steals from you or beats you up you must report them. My brother's best friend came from the Skarzysko Camp and I had known him in Radom as a man with a fine reputation. I asked one of the *blockalteste* to give him a position in his own barrack. He gave him the job of distributing bread and soup. There was usually a good deal of shoving and pushing as people struggled to get their portion as soon as possible. One time the man lost his temper and hit someone with a ladle because the individual had acted too aggressively. His victim, who knew him from before, exploded: "You think you're in Skarzysko where you got away with beating people?"

When I came to the barrack to check on things, the *blockaltester*, Hans, inquired: "Why'd you recommend him?" I asked the accused fellow to tell me his side of the story and he said that the others were jealous that he had gotten such a good job. To find out the truth, the Underground took him to the hospital and held a trial there. Well, he demanded that I be allowed to testify. I told him to get witnesses that could testify on his behalf regarding his behavior in Skarzysko. Yet he was unable to produce any from the hundreds of people that had arrived with him. This upset me greatly. I knew him as a decent person before the war, but you never know how someone will behave under such barbaric conditions. At this point there was nothing I could do to help him.

Many witnesses testified against him and he was found guilty of a number of charges: that he had betrayed Jews to the Germans, and that he constantly cursed, hit, and kicked women in Skarzysko. And so he was found guilty and executed by those who came into the camp with him. Justice was visited upon him by those who suffered at his hands. This was not done simply to take revenge but to insure that this individual would never be in a similar position here.

In another case, a former collaborator ran up to the camp gate and said to the Nazis: "I was a kapo in Skarzysko and I am ready to work for you here." The conversation was overheard by a member of the Underground who reported it to the *blockaltester* in Block 7, which was a barrack for the insane. He, in turn, sent two nurses to the gate who said that the man had escaped from their block. He was taken away and never seen again. The Underground usually won in such matters. They had an excellent network and were highly efficient.

Very few collaborators came out alive from Buchenwald. One who did was a doctor who showed up with his two young sons. He was accused by the people who came with him to Buchenwald of being a collaborator, and they related a terrible story. Five hundred Jews had been taken in his town and quarantined in the synagogue for a month for fear of typhus. The SS called this doctor in and asked him if they were in good health and if they could be sent out to work. He replied: "They're all shit!" Consequently, all of the Jews were pulled out of the synagogue and shot. The doctor was implicated in other killings too; *aktions* where ten, five, or three Jews were murdered. In one case it was alleged that he turned in sixteen Jews who were hiding in a Jewish hospital. To our dismay, the stories were confirmed.

But we, the Jewish cell of the Underground, didn't have so much hatred that we would be willing to punish his children. We felt sorry for them even though the non-Jewish Underground leaders insisted that the collaborator should be liquidated. We told our comrades: "We'll leave him for later." The doctor, like most collaborators, was shrewd and was able to find out who we were. Subsequently he came over to me and said: "Don't believe what they say about me. It's not true." "Why do you come to me?," I said. "Are people mistreating you here?; are you getting less food? I don't want to know what you did elsewhere. It's not my business."

The Underground leadership said: "The children will grow up without him because he is a murderer and he should not come out alive." And although that was the fate of many collaborators, it did not happen to him. We intentionally postponed his case until we were liberated. Suddenly, amidst the chaos, the doctor was forgotten about. Each of us was concerned about his own problems. In my case, I was sick; I had contracted typhus. The nurses had left and the American Red Cross wasn't organized yet. The doctor, who had cheated his own fate, found out that I was sick and he came to my room.

"You know," he said. "I appreciate that you saved my life." I was burning up with fever. And yet, my anger gave me the strength to say:

"Murderer, go away from here. I didn't save your life for your sake, but for the sake of your children." So he said: "I want to help you; I'm a doctor." And I said: "Don't help me. Just leave. I don't want to see you and I don't want your help."

Despite my condition, I refused to be attended to by bloodied hands. Until American medical assistance arrived, my friend, Jack Handelsman brought me aspirin, tea and white bread and saw to my needs. I survived without the help of this doctor who betrayed his humanity and his Hippocratic oath despite his many years of education and enlightenment. And what was his ultimate fate? He came to America and resumed his career as a doctor. He lived a full life and eventually died in Florida. His sons also did very well in this country.

As the Underground's influence increased, its members became bolder. Those assigned to the Gustloff Works began stealing ammunition, as well as engaging in other revolutionary activities. The ammunition was then stored underneath the camp hospital for later use. In December 1942, a major coup was scored by the Underground when it successfully stole a short wave radio. We now had news from Moscow, London, and elsewhere. Amazingly, we were never caught listening to it.

One of the most thrilling moments during my incarceration in Buchenwald occurred on August 24, 1944. In a mere five minutes the "Silver Birds" of the American Air Force completely leveled the Gustloff Works which took us years to build. It was a beautiful sight to watch the planes totally destroy all of the buildings. They also bombed the Nazis' villas outside the gate of the camp. In the process, the stone eagle by the camp gate and the famous Goethe oak tree, under which Goethe supposedly sat, was destroyed. The Germans believed that if this tree ever fell, Germany was doomed. It was amazing to me how such a sophisticated people could be so superstitious; but that was typical of the Germans—full of paradoxes.

Our pleasure at seeing all this was so great that we paid no attention to our personal safety as we stood there and took in the whole scene. There are no words that can adequately express the tremendous joy we felt.

Soon, however, our joy was muted. In revenge for the bombing, the SS shot a large group of prisoners including the leader of the communists, Rudolf Breischeid, a former member of the German Parliament. The official account, however, reported that they had been killed by the American bombs.

As a bricklayer, I volunteered to go out and help repair the damage. I was motivated by curiosity about Ilse Koch's home. I wanted to see the lampshade that had been made from Hans' skin, the fellow who had worked with me on the scaffold.

Well, I got to see it with my own eyes. It was all the more shocking to look at since I had known the man it belonged to so well when he was alive. Underneath the lampshade was a stand made from pieces of human bone and, as a decorative item, a shrunken human skull. The parchment-like material looked like a Torah scroll. You could see the tiny holes where the hair once was. There was also a shrunken head that served as a handle for one of her riding whips.[5] To this day, whenever I think about it, I close my eyes and the lampshade with Hans' tattoos is right there. It is a horrific vision that has always remained with me.

One of the villas I repaired belonged to Dumbock, the cruel Nazi who used to step on peoples' throats in the "garden" where he made them work on Sundays. It was a jarring experience, totally incongruous with what I knew about this vicious man. I walked into his house and he was sitting there in an easy chair with his dog at his side, listening to soft music. He was the very vision of a country gentleman. He was very nice and polite to us, since we were the bricklayers who were going to repair his house. He turned to the Polish maids and said: "Please make sure they have enough to eat." Then, looking at us, he said: "Have a piece of this delicious cake and some coffee." If I hadn't seen his other side, I could have been fooled into being the best witness in his behalf after the war. It was unbelievable that this charming man was the same animal who had the blood of hundreds of Jews on his hands.

By 1944, it was becoming clear that Germany was not doing well in the war. We began to believe in the possibility of Germany losing and started to consider rebellion. Our thinking was that even if we lost, we could at least take some of the Nazis with us as we died.

The Nazis had continually done their best to extinguish any hope we might have had of surviving. "One half-hour before the end, you can be sure we will kill you," they told us repeatedly. This was not merely an empty threat. Corrupt SS men divulged to us that Luftwaffe planes disguised as American aircraft were stationed in nearby Erfurt. Their intended mission was to destroy Buchenwald, killing all of the remaining inmates, and to blame it on the Americans.

Sometimes we thought about escaping but it didn't really make sense. There was no place to escape to because we were in Germany. Some tried but very few got away. In almost all instances they were brought back dead. An electrified barbed wire fence, about two miles long, with 350 volts of current, surrounded the camp and there were guards in twenty-three watch towers. Even if you did somehow make it past the fence, the area right outside was always covered by machine guns located in the towers. And I should mention, in the five and one half years I was there, no one ever attacked or killed a guard. If you could somehow get through the perimeter, where would you run to? Towards the very end, several members of the Underground managed to escape in order to determine the location of the advancing armies. Most were caught, brought back, and hanged.

Escape was not our goal since it was so unrealistic. What we wanted was to survive, to live long enough to tell the world what had happened in Buchenwald. Our desire to do that, however, never really made us afraid of being identified as members of the Underground and reported to the SS. Not that we didn't think it could happen. It was just that we hated the collaborators so much that we didn't care. Caring and worrying would mean that they had succeeded in controlling our actions.

The story of the Underground was one of great heroism and courage in the face of unbelievable odds. Maybe the most remarkable thing is that we continued our activities in the face of great danger over such a long period of time. Probably, it was because our feeling of solidarity was so great that it overcame our own fears.

Notes

1. These were a minority among the Witnesses. On September 6, 1938, the Witnesses were given a chance to purchase their freedom by rejecting their principles in writing. Most did so and were set free. Thus, the remaining ones cited here by Werber were the most steadfast in their beliefs. Eugen Kogon, *The Theory and Practice of Hell*, p. 36.
2. Walter Poller, a political prisoner, notes the case of a Nazi who wore a red triangle. He was considered a political prisoner even though he had been jailed for simple embezzlement of Nazi Party funds. See *Butchers of Buchenwald*, p. 36.
3. Yehoshua R. Buchler, who came to Buchenwald as a child, has described his initial shock at how civilized the people there were. He tells of one old-timer who filled Buchler's cap with food. See *"Block Yeladim 66 BeMachane Ricuz Buchenwald,"* ("Childrens' Block 66 in Buchenwald Concentration Camp.") in *Yalkut Moreshet*, 25, No. 1, April 1978, English translation, p. 3.
4. In the last three months of Buchenwald's existence, there were 13,066 recorded deaths. See Gerald Reitlinger, *The Final Solution* (rev. ed.). Cranberry, N.J.: Thomas Yosseloff, 1968:498.
5. See Kogon, pp. 228–229.

7

Saving the Children

The period right before the war was a very happy one for me personally. This despite the international turmoil, uncertainty for Jews in Poland, and my deferred dreams of settling in Palestine. I was happily married and had a daughter that I absolutely adored. When I was arrested, our baby was fourteen months old. And you can imagine what went through my mind. Certainly not that I would go into a gas chamber, for at that time we couldn't even imagine such a thing. I was worried about my wife and child. How would they support themselves if I wasn't there? Every day the Nazis were coming out with new laws that made life more difficult.

Of course, I had no idea that every member of my family would be brutally murdered. I learned the awful truth about their fate during my imprisonment in Buchenwald. To this day, I remember clearly how it happened.

Early one morning, in the beginning of 1944, I stood on the *appelplatz*, lined up in formation. It was still dark and a blanket of thick fog covered the area. The cold air penetrated our very bones and we stood there shivering, trying to get a little warmer by standing close, rubbing each other's backs, as well as our own frozen fingers.

As it grew lighter and the morning mist began to lift, we heard the *rapportführer's* announcement through the loudspeaker: "*Arbeits commandos antraten* " (Work details, fall in). Thousands of inmates began running like ants in every direction. I headed towards my own commando, the bricklayers' detail, a few hundred feet away.

Suddenly a man, his face swollen and covered with bruises, grabbed my arm, and screamed, in a wild, unnatural voice:

"Jakub? You are alive? Your father buried your ashes in the Jewish cemetery!" His face was hardly recognizable, but after staring at him for a moment, it came to me. It was Solohub, our good Ukrainian neighbor from Radom. His father was an Eastern Orthodox cleric and his wife was a Jewish doctor, whose father was a rabbi. Looking at him, standing here on the *appelplatz*, I was momentarily stunned. All I could say was:

"Which barrack are you in?"

"Forty-three," he answered.

"I'll see you after the evening *appel*," I told him, moving away to join my group for work.

That day was perhaps the longest day of my life in the camp. I couldn't take my mind off what had happened. What would he tell me about my family when I saw him again?, I wondered. Why did they bury my ashes when I'm still alive? Due to my nervousness everything went wrong that day. I couldn't concentrate on my work and made numerous mistakes.

"What's wrong with you?" said the kapo, Siewert. "You're one of the best bricklayers around here. Yet you seem so confused."

"I don't feel so well," I answered.

"Okay," he responded. "Starting tomorrow you'll work indoors for a few days, in the machinery hall, fixing the cement floor. You won't be so visible to the SS over there."

To make matters harder, the *appel* that evening took even longer than usual. We were forced to sing the Buchenwald *Lied* for over an hour and when the rest of the inmates finally marched back to the barrack, we Jews had to remain and sing the *Juden Lied* for another hour. All I could think about was seeing Solohub. I didn't even bother to eat the soup. I just grabbed my *zullage* (extra portion of bread which we were entitled to as bricklayers) to give to Solohub and left immediately for his barrack.

When I got there, Solohub was waiting by the door. The *blockaltester* was also there, apparently telling him it was time to go inside for the night. Fortunately, the *blockaltester* was a friend of mine from my days in the quarry and I was able to convince him to leave Solohub alone with me. With tears in his eyes, Solohub began telling me what had happened to my family.

A few months after my arrest my father was summoned to the *Judenrat* headquarters. When he arrived he was told that I had died of dysentery and that, for a considerable fee, the ashes would be sent to him. He paid the money, some outrageous sum, and buried the ashes according to Jewish law in the Radom Jewish cemetery.

My father never recovered from this tragedy, according to Solohub. The pain of losing his youngest son was just too much to bear and, a few months later, he died.

"What about the rest of my family?," I asked, afraid of the answer even as I did so.

"Everybody is gone," he answered sadly.

So that was it. My wife, Rachel, and my three-year-old daughter, Emma, were dead. And so were my brothers and sisters and their children. Solohub informed me that they had all been deported and gassed in Treblinka except for my niece Fela and my nephew, Zyniek, who had escaped from the ghetto. I couldn't believe, even then, that they just gassed innocent children. Buchenwald, terrible as it was, had no gas chambers. Solohub filled in the details for me.

The Germans established a Jewish ghetto in Radom in 1942. People were crowded into very small areas—two or three families to a room. They were used every day for slave labor and given no food. It was a real hell. Piles of corpses lay in the streets every day, dead from starvation and epidemics. People sold their personal belongings in order to buy food that had been smuggled in from outside the ghetto. Many were caught doing so and shot on the spot.

Eventually, the ghetto was emptied out. With the exception of 2,000 Jews who worked in the ammunition factory, the rest of the Jewish population, about 30,000 souls, was transported to Treblinka. They marched to their deaths, with a towel and a bar of soap, thinking they were going to the showers. After being gassed, their bodies were burnt in the crematoria.

When Solohub finished, I looked at him in horror and disbelief. I simply couldn't believe what he had told me. That night I couldn't sleep at all, not even for a moment. I just lay awake and tried to make sense of everything I had heard. I was suspicious that maybe Solohub was simply telling me a story to get favors from me.

The next day at work, I repeated what Solohub had told me, to Elek Greenbaum, the *stubedienst*, and to Emil Carlebach. They agreed with me that such a thing was not possible, that even the Nazis would not be so barbaric as to simply exterminate millions of men, women, and children, just for the crime of having been born Jewish.

Nevertheless, I couldn't forget the story, not for months afterward. And in the back of my mind I kept wondering if maybe it was true. After all, how could you even make up something like that? And I knew Solohub to be an honorable and trustworthy person who would not lie just to get food or a better job in the camp.

Because I felt this way, I succeeded in getting Solohub transferred from the quarry to the *Bau* Commando, where he worked as a helper. I also saw to it that he got extra food whenever possible.

Nightmares about what happened to my family became a regular part of my life. I hoped and prayed that what Solohub had said wasn't true. But it was no use; I had become a different person.

In the middle of 1944, a transport of Jews arrived in Buchenwald. Some of them were from Radom and they confirmed the tragic events related by Solohub. There had been deportations and mass gassings at Treblinka, including old people and infants. I also learned about other extermination centers—Auschwitz, Belzec, Sobibor, and Chelmno, and I was filled with dread.

I fell into a deep depression and lost all faith and hope. I felt that I no longer had anything to live for. My sadness was so great that I found it almost impossible to function on a daily basis. I said to myself that I had nobody to care about, so why go on? For whom? My friends, seeing the change in my behavior, tried to comfort me and give me reasons to go on. "We must live to see the end of Nazism," they said. "We must take revenge and if we must die, then let us die in battle with the Nazis."

I heard what they had to say, but it didn't really help me. Nothing helped, that is, until the children came to Buchenwald.

Most of the youngsters arrived in August of 1944, primarily from the Skarzysko Camp, mixed in with a larger group of more than 2,000 prisoners. Some came with their fathers, others had no fathers or had been separated from them. They ranged in age from six to sixteen, with most between thirteen and fifteen. Altogether, the group numbered about 700 boys.

Seeing them instantly brought to mind what had happened to my own child. I decided to get involved, to see if I could do something to help them avoid the fate of my own beloved Emma.

I also remembered what had happened to an earlier transport of Gypsy children when the criminals were still in power in the camp. They had been transferred to an unknown destination and we assumed they wound up dead. I knew that if nothing was done, these children would meet the same end.

Miraculously, we were able to save most of them. A few, unfortunately, were taken away with other transports, to Bergen-Belsen and elsewhere, usually because they wanted to go with their fathers, or other relatives, and not be left behind in Buchenwald. We felt terrible about that, but what could we do? We had to act fast because the transport trains were only supposed to make brief stops in Buchenwald en route to other destinations.

How was it possible to save any children at all? It's incomprehensible that a small band of feeble inmates could keep such a deception from their oppressors. It just doesn't seem plausible that we could get away with housing, feeding and protecting close to seven hundred children under the noses of the Nazis. And yet we did.

This miracle came about through the fortunate convergence of several factors. The organizational structure created by the Nazis required a minimal number of German officers. The responsibility for the day to day running of the camp was delegated to inmates, who by the end of the war were mainly Underground operatives. Buchenwald was a work camp for political prisoners, and not primarily an extermination camp for Jews. Accordingly, inmates were given a bit more leeway both in terms of their movement and in receiving packages from the outside, than in other camps. Furthermore, by the last few months of the war, as the threat of defeat loomed more ominously, the German officers became more concerned about their personal safety than with what was going on in Buchenwald. They abdicated more and more control of the camp, and rarely entered the barracks.

With the consent of my supervisor from the Underground, Emil Carlebach, I called a meeting of Jewish members of the Underground—Jack Handelsman, Elek Greenbaum, and Gustav Schiller, among others.

At the meeting we agreed that if the accounts of what was happening to European Jewry were true, then it was crucial that we do something positive and important. These boys, due to the nature of camp life, grew up literally overnight. They had to, in order to protect themselves.[1] A typical ten year old saw death almost every day. Our task was to save their lives and to give them hope for the future, even though we ourselves were often despairing.

The general non-Jewish Underground did not oppose our efforts to save the children, although for them this wasn't a priority like saving politicals or those with military skills. Some even thought that the children shouldn't be in Buchenwald because it was so difficult to hide them. I guess you could say that we arrived at a gentlemen's agreement that they wouldn't mix into our business and that we would continue to cooperate with the Underground on general problems. They didn't strenuously insist upon their position because I believe they wanted to maintain the coalition with the Jews.

Our Jewish group was only one part of the Underground but rescuing the children was our pet project and we took the lead in this matter. We saw it as our duty, with or without Underground support, to save as many children as possible. I met with Hans, Johann, and Emil, general Underground leaders, and sought and obtained their agreement to use the methods we had developed earlier to obtain extra food for the children. This food was to come, willingly or under pressure, from the German prisoners and Jewish prisoners who had German wives and who received packages from home.

We also asked for help in obtaining assistance from the *schreibstube*, the office secretaries. They changed the birth dates of the children so that they would be listed as older and therefore eligible to work. To "legally" keep them in the camp children had to be assigned to a work detail. And officially, you had to be sixteen to remain in Buchenwald. For those who were of that age we didn't have to change the date.

Finally, we pointed out to the Underground that the SS was losing control of the camp and that we, the Jewish underground members, would take full responsibility for the welfare of the children. I explained that our main fear was that if we did not take drastic action, the children would be sent to their deaths. I conceded that it was an enormous undertaking to protect the children who had no official standing or "right" to be there, for they were too young to be in a labor camp. I concluded my appeal with the following words: "Look, it's a risk, but maybe the children will survive by some miracle, so let's take the chance and try to save them."

After a week, Emil told me that the Underground had agreed to our plan.

Those who were most involved with me in our efforts to help the children were Gustav Schiller, Jack Handelsman, and Elek Greenbaum. Schiller was actually a real mystery to me, in terms of his motives. He was, what you would call, "a real rough guy." Rumor had it that in prewar Germany he had been part of the criminal underworld. Nevertheless, "the children" who survived remember Schiller, the deputy *blockaltester* of Block 66, with fondness.

My own job, as barrack secretary, enabled me to care for the 150 or so children in Block 23 on a daily basis and I did this for about ten months, until the war ended. Suffering a great personal loss drove me in my obsession to save children. I saw each one of them as if he were my own.

The two people who helped me the most in this undertaking were Jack Handelsman, the *stubedienst* of Wing A, and Elek Greenbaum, *stubedienst* of Wing B. Together with them I organized food for the children, much of it by way of people who worked outside the camp and had extra. The kitchen kapo belonged to the Underground and he also set aside food for the youngsters. Quite a few of the blocks had special bowls or baskets into which inmates put scraps of bread; most didn't know that it was going to the children. The leader of Block 23 was Karl Siegmeyer, a German communist from Leipzig. Calling him a good person isn't adequate. He was a saint. Hans Reines was the deputy block leader. He was an assimilated Czech Jew and also an outstanding individual.

Unfortunately, we sometimes encountered inmates unwilling to give up their packages for the children, even if they had enough to eat. I remember one fellow who had a very rich German friend who sent him nice packages. He refused to give anything to anyone else. We had no option but to force him share the food. Now I'm sure that if I were to meet him today he would say we were very mean to him. A reader of this account might even ask what right we had to take away his property. Both responses reflect a lack of comprehension of the reality we faced in Buchenwald. This inmate failed to appreciate how good he had it in 1944, even without the packages, compared with the earlier years, and compared to the hardship and suffering endured by the children.

We were also able to get food from the medical block because two Jews who worked there gave us the extra food that those who became sick from the experiments and were unable to eat. Additional rations were secured by giving the Nazis higher counts of inmates. This was accomplished by not reporting right away those who had died. In doing so we were able to get extra loaves of bread.

Clothing was much harder to secure because there wasn't any that could fit the smaller ones since Buchenwald was a mens' camp.

There was no choice but for many of the younger children to wear the same clothes for weeks on end and to just try to stay as clean as possible. Most remained dressed in civilian clothes because near the end the camp had no prison uniforms for new inmates.

Most importantly, I tried to give the children love and compassion. This was crucial because the majority no longer had living parents. The very act of doing this gave my life meaning.

Our strategy on where to house the children shifted frequently, in response to what seemed like the right thing to do at the time. Even after we made a decision, we weren't certain it was the correct one. Sometimes it seemed to make more sense to keep certain children together and at other times we thought it prudent to break them up into smaller groups and disperse them among more barracks. Our information about the plans of the SS was limited, often based on the reports of SS officers we were able to bribe or merely rumors.

The decision was made to scatter the children into different barracks. The majority went into the Small Camp, which was an enclosed area on the side of the larger camp. The Small Camp was used by the Nazis as a temporary location for prisoners who were to be shipped either to other work sites or to their deaths. Accordingly, inmates in the Small Camp were not required to work and we didn't have to find jobs for the children placed there. They were housed in Block 66, a wooden barrack which eventually became an all-childrens' block, under the leadership of a Czech political prisoner.

Elie Wiesel, Rabbi Israel Lau, the Chief Rabbi of Israel, and his brother, Naftali Lavi, who was an Israeli diplomat, were also in this block. Of course, we had no idea at the time who they would become. They were simply part of a larger group of children whose lives we helped save.

Some of the prisoners who took care of them were non-Jewish politicals, including a highly respected humanitarian, who was the *blockaltester*. They worked with the Jewish deputy block leader, Gustav Schiller and the *stubedienst*, Baruch Goldberg. Gustav made sure that the food was given out fairly and he also spent a great deal of time with the children, who came to him with their problems.[2] On the other hand, he was very strict and quite capable of losing his temper. Whenever this happened, I was called upon, in the name of the Underground, to put him in his place. It was something I did only reluctantly, because I knew his heart was in the right place and that he, like the rest of our group, was ready to sacrifice his life for the sake of the children.

The rest of the youngsters were placed mainly in Barracks 23, 22, and 8. These had not only children but also adults. When the situation became too dangerous in one place, the children would be shifted to another barrack. There were also smaller groups of children scattered throughout various other blocks. The children were suspicious, however. They were afraid that being broken up into small groups was a trick to get them to participate in medical experiments. This wasn't so surprising because, in other camps, whenever children under sixteen years of age were put into a separate group it meant that they were too young to work and would therefore be killed.

We were reluctant to have too many of them transferred into the larger camp because we were afraid that we wouldn't be able to find work for them there. The older children who could pass for sixteen were assigned to work commandos. Whenever possible we had the children assigned to indoor commandos where it was easier, such as electricians' helpers. Cooperative inmates, who worked as clerks, listed some of the younger children as being assigned to work commandos. These entries were fictitious and the children never actually worked.

Conditions in the Small Camp were far worse than in the big camp where everyone at least had his own bunk. It was a real dilemma and we tried to manage as best we could. For example, we were sometimes able to arrange for the roll call in the Small Camp to be held indoors, which meant that the youngsters were not exposed to terrible cold and snow in the winter.

Providing food, while crucial, was not enough to sustain the children, most of whom spoke only Yiddish and, or Polish. The challenge for us was to keep them alive, mentally and spiritually. Because of the terrible things they had seen, the children were more like old people. To achieve this goal our group held a meeting and decided to set up a school for them. We also discussed how we would persuade the Underground not to oppose our efforts. Finally, we identified people that we felt we could approach to teach the children. We needed people who were not only capable and trustworthy, but who were also willing to risk their lives in this activity. Baruch Goldberg was instrumental in recruiting our faculty. He had come on the same transport as some of the people whom we eventually chose. We explained to these individuals that this was dangerous work and that they might lose their lives if they were caught. It was a testament to the courage and dedication of those selected that they were willing to assume these risks.

One of those asked to teach them reading and writing was Mordechai Strigler, now the editor of the Yiddish *Forward* in New York. Strigler, a former yeshiva student, was greatly respected as a teacher and as a writer. Strigler gave the children hope by telling them stories of Jewish resistance and courage in the past and promised that one day they would have revenge against their tormentors. But it wasn't always easy. One eight year old refused to go to classes. He asked: "Why should I go to school? I won't come out alive anyway." Such cynicism on the part of the young was certainly understandable, and hard to refute. There were many other children who shared this little child's sense of hopelessness.

On our "faculty" was a violinist, Brandt. The Buchenwald storage facility housed all of the belongings confiscated from new arrivals: crutches, eyeglasses, whatever they considered precious. We took a violin from there and gave it to Brandt. The children loved to hear him play Jewish songs for them. David Neumann had a beautiful voice and he gave the children singing instruction. Meir Gottlieb was the drama instructor and he also taught Jewish subjects. Among the topics taught were history, Yiddish songs, and Hebrew language. Obviously, everything was done without books, just from memory. So people like Strigler and Gottlieb would reconstruct poetry by Bialik, Gebirtig, Ahad Ha'Am, and Peretz as best as they could remember. Handelsman and I told them stories designed to give them hope, about how after the war we would all go to Palestine and grow oranges in a Jewish country. To keep up their spirits, we would teach them Hebrew songs that we remembered from our days in Hashomer Hatzair.

All this led up to choir performances, plays, and poetry readings. The children stood up and acted, usually on top of several tables that we had put together. On several occasions, we invited non-Jewish members of the Underground to the performances, just so they should see that we were really giving the children an education. Sure, they trusted us, but it's important to understand that in these circumstances people sometimes got a little paranoid. And there was another problem. We were concerned that if we emphasized Jewish culture too much, the Underground would see it as anticommunist and against the spirit of international brotherhood. Conducting these classes was exceedingly dangerous. On several occasions when the SS unexpectedly approached the barrack, we had to evacuate the younger children through the windows.

Actually, there was one block in which two opposing educational approaches were used at the same time. In Barrack 8, the Russian communists had set up a program for Russian children. Everything taught was according to Communist Party dogma. But there were also Jewish kids from the Carpathian Mountains in Barrack 8 who were taught about the Jewish religion and Zionism by Israel Rob. As far as I know the two groups didn't mix together.

Incredible as it sounds, we actually had a schoolroom in Buchenwald, in the regular camp, complete with blackboards, paper, etc. It began in September, 1944, and met an average of three times a week. The "classroom" was in Barrack 23 and the blackboard was made from a piece of wood that had been painted black. We used empty cement bags as writing paper for the children. If the Germans approached, our own guards would yell "eighteen" and they would have to destroy the paper and hide their pencils. Usually, the "students" sat on the bunk beds facing the center of the room, making certain not to bang their heads on the bunk beds above them. Although the children in Barrack 66 didn't receive any of this Jewish education, there were public performances at which they sang Jewish songs, while other nationalities also made similar presentations.

I held on to my official job as a secretary in Barrack 23, so that I could continue working with the children. It wasn't exactly a nine to five job. New problems came up every day. We were, out of necessity, amateur psychologists. We had to deal with the needs of children traumatized by war, deprived of parental affection, and old beyond their years. We tried to give them hope that there would be a tomorrow. We would ask them what they wanted to be when they got older. Some wanted to be doctors and others policemen. Not surprisingly, most of the boys, having lost their families, deprived of their youth, and now imprisoned in a concentration camp, were very skeptical that they would ever get the chance to be anything. But even if they thought of this as a fantasy, dreaming about future careers helped pass the time and took their minds, ever so briefly, off the nightmare they were living in the camp.

The children were almost always kept inside the barracks. We were lucky that the SS men were so busy trying to avoid being sent to the Russian Front that they weren't able to pay close attention to everything that we were doing.

When the SS wanted to inspect the Small Camp, they were told all sorts of stories to prevent them from doing so. The most common excuse was that, with people coming from all over, there was a risk of epidemics, something that the Nazis were truly afraid of. And since the Small Camp was only a temporary place, a warehousing operation, the SS didn't bother too much with examining the arrivals for disease. When this argument failed and they showed up anyway, we pulled out all of the sixteen year olds and gave them jobs to do. The foreman would then scream at them, for the benefit of the SS—"Work harder! You eat for nothing! We give you food!" For some we got phony notes from the hospital stating that they were ill and had to stay indoors. As time went by, the problem of keeping the children out of the sight of the SS became more complicated because the kids, especially the younger ones, felt more secure and started running around in the open. Often, it was necessary to move the youngsters from one barrack to the next, on very short notice.

The Nazi attempts to destroy our movement continued right up to the end of the war. However, as the end drew near, the relationship between the SS and the politicals changed because our captors realized we might be exchanging places and that they would need the politicals as witnesses on their behalf. On April 3rd, the Camp Commander, Herman Pister, made a speech in which he spoke directly, for the first time, to the prisoner leaders. This was unusual because, by and large, the only direct communications between the top camp officials and the inmate population were the orders given by the SS over the public address system. We were assembled in the camp movie theater, where the *commandant* said: "We know that you have ammunition. We know everything that you're doing. But don't provoke us. And if you don't revolt, I give you my word as a soldier to turn over the entire camp to the Americans at the end." Of course, we didn't trust them. We continued with our preparations and laid out earthenware white plates on a tar roof background, in a pattern spelling out the letters S-O-S. After the liberation, American fliers told us they had indeed seen the signal.

Two days later the Nazis told the *lageralteste* that they wanted to evacuate the entire camp "to protect us from the Americans." Our leaders protested: "But you gave your word that you'd turn over the camp, with us in it, to the Americans." Well, they had changed their minds. They said that this was an order from Berlin. So we bargained with them. The camp population was now down to under 60,000 inmates. We tried everything possible to reduce the number of people to be evacuated and to delay the process. Our hope was that the Allies would liberate the camp before the Nazis could remove the prisoners. We told the SS that we needed more time to prepare the lists of evacuees. So we got them to postpone the evacuation initially for a day or two, and to reduce it from 10,000 to less than 5,000 inmates a day.[3]

In reality, the Underground was not certain whether or not to leave the camp. We knew from SS men who collaborated with us that the Nazis had a secret plan to use planes with phony American markings to bombard and destroy Buchenwald if it appeared that all was lost. The planes were located at Nora Airfield in nearby Erfurt. In this way, the Americans would be blamed for our deaths. For this reason, some felt that remaining in the camp would be a mistake. Others believed that if they stalled, the Americans would come and rescue the inmates before the Nazis had a chance to carry out their plan.

We decided that if they tried to evacuate the whole camp we would fight. We realized that we couldn't win since we were in the middle of Germany but we didn't want to die without resisting and without defending the children. Under no circumstances would we give up the children.

The SS was particularly interested in removing the Jews from the camp. To respond to this threat, the Underground held a meeting. It was decided that when they ordered all of the Jews to step out at roll call on the *appelplatz*, the Jews would disobey the order. Instead they would blend in with everyone else and hide.[4] And this is precisely what happened.

The Nazis became enraged and demanded that the *lageralteste* identify the Jews. The *lageralteste* defied the order, however, and said to the Germans: "Go find them yourselves." The Nazis responded by arresting the head *lageraltester* and threw him into the "bunker." The "bunker" was a cell the size of a telephone booth and was located in a basement. Water came out of the walls steadily and the incarcerated got no food. I knew how unpleasant this punishment was through personal experience. Due to a case of mistaken identity, I was once put into the bunker for three days. The SS wanted to punish a German inmate whose number was similar to mine. A couple of digits were transposed in the punishment order, and I wound up in the bunker instead.

Despite this, the prisoners refused to give in. The deputy head *lageraltester* also refused to single out the Jews and he too was tossed into the bunker. The Nazis finally gave up.[5] As a further precaution, my number and those of the other Jews in the Underground were all declared dead by the hospital. We were given fictitious numbers so that we would have new identities. From then on, we no longer went out to work.

There were, however, some final Jewish victims of this last *appel*. So deep was the German hatred for Jews that even as they saw defeat on the horizon, they hastened their efforts to slaughter more of us. A transport of half-dead, Jewish new arrivals were off to one side of the *appelplatz*. They had no idea what was going on. The SS removed these poor unfortunates from the area and shot them outside the main camp. After the liberation, we found their corpses piled up by the hundreds.

We were heading towards anarchy in the camp. We didn't know what would be, and so we tried planning for all contingencies, constantly changing strategies as new possibilities entered our minds. We learned the SS had a list of fifty-seven politicals that were to be killed before they gave up the camp. To stop them the politicals were hidden in a bunker secretly dug beforehand by the Underground.

The Jewish cell of the Underground had prepared another bunker a few weeks earlier, next to the childrens' block in the Small Camp. We stocked it with bottles of water and food. We thought that if the children were to be evacuated we would go with them on the transport. But if the SS were to seek only the Jewish leaders, we would hide in the bunker.

At Emil Carlebach's suggestion, I went to the Small Camp with Handelsman to check on the children. We had to mix in together with other adults in a nearby barrack in order to find out what was going on. There were thousands of people in the Small Camp and conditions were awful. The Hungarian Jews, in particular, suffered terribly. Many had only recently come to the camps for the first time and weren't used to the hard life. As a result, they were more likely to fall apart. The few Greek Jews that were there also didn't fare well. They died almost immediately because they were unaccustomed to the freezing weather.

That night we found ourselves with a bunch of rough guys, Ukrainians, who attacked Handelsman and me. For security reasons we couldn't even tell them that we were with the Underground. So to them we were just Jewish inmates. We decided to stay in the barrack so that we could gather the information about the status of the children as planned.

In the morning, we volunteered to go to the kitchen in the big camp to get coffee for everyone and to learn what had happened there overnight. When we arrived, we discovered that our fellow inmates in all—Jewish Barrack 23, fearing evacuation, had left and scattered elsewhere throughout the camp.

The last few days were chaotic as more and more prisoners began to defy orders. People were running from one place to another trying to hide from the SS. On April 4th, the daily morning roll calls stopped. It was clear that the end was near. We decided that we would fight with our fists, if necessary, to save our lives.

On April 9th the Underground met to discuss when to begin the uprising. Some wanted to act immediately but the majority favored postponing taking any action. They felt that with 3,000 fully armed SS men still in the camp area, our chances of success were very small. That same night twenty-four political prisoners were murdered by the Nazis as well as sixteen SS men who tried to desert their unit.

The hospital became a hiding place for some political prisoners whom the Nazis had decided to liquidate. In some instances, these men were listed as having died in the hospital and then simply given new names. Sometimes they were even put in TB wards because the Nazis were terrified of catching TB and never entered those parts of the hospital.

April 11, 1945, dawned bright and clear. Compared to the nerve-racking days of the past two weeks it was strangely quiet—no roll call, no transports, just silence. I felt as though something was going to happen, and I didn't have long to wait. One of the Underground leaders told us to gather by the lower part of the camp, behind the hospital. Using binoculars stolen from the Germans, we could see the American tanks coming closer and could hear the sounds of artillery growing louder.

At 11:00 A.M. the emergency sirens sounded, but we ignored them. Shortly afterwards, we heard an electrifying announcement from the *rapportführer*: "All SS officers, leave the camp." We became very excited. It was clear that our freedom was near. This wretched place, which had held more than 238,000 prisoners through the years, would soon cease to exist. We listened eagerly to the radio as the BBC described the bombings of Hamburg, Bremen, and other cities of what the Germans had called "The One Thousand Year Reich."

At this point, the Underground went into action. The leaders removed a cache of weapons that they had acquired through the years from a hiding place beneath the hospital complex. According to published accounts, it included 1,500 rifles and guns, 180 hand grenades, 18 light machine guns, and 4 heavy machine guns.[6] Everyone was given an assignment. The Camp Police, which was trained for military action, became our combat unit. Around 1:00 P.M., the order was given to begin fighting.

I was part of a two-man team whose job it was to cut the wires and create openings of about six feet, so that the Underground fighters could get out and attack the Germans. We were positioned to the left of the main gate. According to the plan, the breaking of the perimeter was to be carried out at the same time at numerous locations along the fence that surrounded the camp, especially near the main gate, the towers, and by the area that controlled the camp's electricity. We used scissors wrapped with ropes so as not to get electrocuted. As soon as the wires were cut, the fighters dashed through the openings and began attacking. They stormed the SS living quarters and also cut the wires that provided electrical power to the camp fence. They also took whatever food they could find and brought it to the camp kitchen for the inmates.

Armed with machine guns, several of our men entered the gate office. As they came in, they saw an SS officer with his back to them. He was shouting into the phone:

"Send help right away! The camp is under attack! Commandant Pister has already left. He tried to call the Nora Airfield for the planes you promised and couldn't get through. You were supposed to send reinforcements hours ago! Soon it will be too late."

"It *is* too late," said one of our men. Upon hearing his voice, the officer whirled around and found himself staring into the sights of several machine guns. Without saying a word, he threw up his hands and surrendered.

The Germans had placed the Ukrainian guards in charge of the watchtowers and I would say they were just as vicious as the Germans, if not worse. But they didn't stay in the watchtowers for very long. They removed their uniforms and put on civilian clothes so that they would be inconspicuous and get away. But we recognized and killed most of them. The few who were able to get away and ran into the forest didn't get very far. They were shot by our people.

While some of the SS officers were still in Buchenwald, a German army flame-throwing unit arrived with special orders to destroy the camp and all those still in it. They were very surprised to see us there. The Underground killed several of them, disarmed the rest, and took away their weapons. By 3:15 P.M., the battle was over. The clock in the watch tower was stopped, to be a permanent reminder of the moment of liberation. A white flag now flew from the tower by the gate. Freedom had come at last for the 21,000 remaining Buchenwald inmates. No more hangings, whippings, beatings and other forms of torture; no more hunger and thirst. Finally, we were able to come and go as we pleased. Many Nazis were dead, and most had surrendered. All told, we captured 220 SS men who were then put under guard in Barrack 17. Our own casualties were very light—two dead and several more wounded. Our commander announced over the microphone:

"The camp has been liberated. You are all free, but please do not leave your barrack until further instructions." We survived to give witness to the greatest act of barbarity in human history, one executed by the "most civilized" nation on earth. But most important, we managed to save nearly 700 children who had miraculously survived in the heart of the Nazi death machine.

Notes

1. For more on this see Richard C. Lukas, *Did the Children Cry?* New York: Hippocrane, 1994:203-204. For detailed accounts of what happened to the children in Buchenwald see Ruczka Korczak, *"Yeladim BeMachane Ricuz Buchenwald,"* ("Children in Buchenwald Concentration Camp") in *Yalkut Moreshet*, 8, No. 1, March 1968, pp. 42-74.
2. For more on Schiller's central role in helping the children see Yehoshua R. Buchler, *"Block Yeladim 66 BeMachane Ricuz Buchenwald,"* p. 7.
3. 28,285 prisoners were evacuated between April 3-10, 1945. See Gerald Reitlinger, *the Final Solution*, p. 505.
4. See Elie Wiesel, *Night*. New York: Bantam paperback edition, 1986, p. 108.
5. According to Kogon, Himmler had ordered on April 2nd that no Jew should be killed. This was ostensibly for political reasons since the war, at that point, seemed to be lost. *The Theory and Practice of Hell*, p. 262.
6. See Emil Carlebach, Paul Grunewald, *et al, Buchenwald: Ein Konzentrationslager.* Berlin: Dietz Verlag, 1988:147.

8

Free At Last

By evening, the first American tanks had arrived at Buchenwald. Our leaders greeted the Americans at the gate and showed them around. Satisfied that the Underground was firmly in control of the camp, the Americans left for Weimar to continue their military operations. It's important to stress that, contrary to popular opinion, it was the Underground, and not the U.S. Army, that liberated the camp (see figure 1).

On April 12th, we gathered on the *appelplatz* to celebrate our liberation. The following day, the American Army returned in full force, together with nurses, doctors, and other support people. They brought with them all sorts of supplies—medicine, cots, food, and so on and ordered us to turn over to them both our weapons and our prisoners.

Two days after liberation, we went to Weimar and forced the Mayor to come to Buchenwald and to bring with him the local population to see what the camp had really been like. When they came they were greeted by a large sign that we had prepared, carried by the children of Buchenwald. It read: "Where are our parents?" They looked at everything—how the hundreds upon hundreds of dead bodies were piled up—and acted shocked, but I had the feeling that a lot of them just pretended not to know what was happening in Buchenwald, only five miles from their homes.

We took the children out of the camp and put them into the nearby SS quarters where there were comfortable beds, dressers, tables, and hot showers. Rabbi Herschel Marcus, who had come in with the

FIGURE 1
Modern Military Archives, Washington
Fourth Armored Division, 604-2.2-daily reports
June 1944–May 1949

HQ'S 4TH ARMD DIV
A.P.O. 254, U.S. ARMY

FROM: 121600B Apr 45
TO : 131600B Apr 45
PLACE: GOTTERN (J6262) GERMANY

G - 2   J O U R N A L

TO	FROM	TIME RECD	TIME SIGNED	SI NO.	INCIDENTS, MSGS, ORDERS, ETC.
C	CG 4 AD		1800	12	Be prepared to cross CCA by 0600B tomorrow. Area to move to will be sent later.
2	IPW 56	1800	1115	13	33 PW's captd N of JENA: CT SCHMIDT 4, 1 PzGr Bn 16, SS Guards BUCHENHAL 3, misc stragglers 10, CT SCHMIDT composed of stragglers collected in WEIMAR on 11 April. Inf weapons strength unknown. Concentration camp BUCHENWALD (L775) occupied by 21400 political prisoners: about 7000 French. Others are German anti-Nazis, Russians, Poles, Spaniards. About 20,000 have been evacuated during past 3 days. Medical Sit: 3,000 sick, many in critical state; 3,000 invalids incl blind. Hospital and doctors present but no medicine or med materials or desinfectants on hand. No operations can be made. Situation desperate. Help urgently required. Food Sit: sufficient for 2 days but no bread at all on hand - special assault groups had been organized to over-power the guards. Before our arrival the guard posts were taken and 125 SS were captd and are still in the custody of the camp. The leadership of the camp is in the hands of a well organized committee comprising all nationalities represented. 32 PW's captd betn DENSTEDT (5673) and MOHLSTEDT (6369): Identifications: CT ZIRKEL 14, 33 AA Repl Bn, WEIMAR 2, 1st Pz Gr Repl Bn 6, 279 Army AA Tng Bn 4, CT KORNINGS 1, misc stragglers 5. PW Statements: CT ZIRKEL: consisting at approx 100 men w/ing weapons committed 11 Apr DENSTEDT (5773) under Capt ZIRKEL. Men are stragglers and hospital cases picked up in WEIMAR on 10 Apr. 33 AA Tng Bn: Bn combined into a alarm Co of 120 men. C.O. 1st Lt FREDERSDORF.
ext	G-2 Curtis	1800	0145	14	TO: CG, 4 AD, CG 6 AD, CG 76 ID, CG 80 ID, CO 3rd Cav Op. Higher Hq requests any available info re man identified only as BLANKENHORST - believed captured vic EISENACH (H7067).
2	OB 24	1800	1800	15	GERMAN DIVS OPERATING CENTRAL SECTOR RUSSIAN FRONT AVAILABLE FOR COMMITMENT AGAINST XX U S CORPS: Fourth Panzer Army (LEIPZIG * CHEMNITZ - DRESDEN - TORGAU area): 21 Pz Div, 25 PGD, 74, 88, 173, 174, 214, 253, 269, 291, 320, 342, 359, 561 Inf Divs, 100 Lt Div. First Panzer Army (operating area N from PRAGUE to Fourth Panzer Army zone): 16 Pz Div, 10 Pz Gr Div, 18 SS Pz Gr Div, 20 Pz Gr Div, 17, 68, 72, 96, 154, 168, 208, 252, 253, 254, 540 Inf Divs, 97 Lt Div.
2	Lt Desard	1800	1100	16	French PW of ISSERSTEDT 65-69 reports: Germans organized resistance bank E of SAALE - would have some artillery - yesterday 1600 - 2 guns pull tractor double gun of 88 on each chassis coupled - coming WEIMAR going to TENA - TN ROTHENSTEIN (7257) important underground plane factory (new type turbing) - near HERMODORFF (63-90) very important ammunition dump (underground).

Americans, brought truckloads of clothing for the kids, as well as for everyone else. Rabbi Herschel Schachter arrived on the scene a little later and brought *tefilin*, prayer books, and other religious articles. Some of the children left on their own to nearby towns to learn how to manage in the world as orphans. They were expecting to go to Palestine and so they set up a community where they could prepare for that eventuality, and named it Kibbutz Buchenwald.

Later, most of the children were taken to France and Switzerland by Jewish organizations. I didn't go with the children for several reasons. First, I was too weak to go anywhere. Second, I wanted to eventually return to Radom to see if my brother Daniel's children, Zyniek and Fela, had come back to their home. Most importantly, I felt that the children were now in good hands. I had done my job. It has always been a tremendous comfort to me that I participated in this effort. It's ironic that such a meaningful period in my life occurred under such dire conditions, when I was a prisoner in a concentration camp.

Over the years I have met many children from this group. Once I was walking in Paris and a blonde fellow, over six feet tall, came up and hugged me. He recognized me from Buchenwald. Another time, a child survivor from Block 23 recognized me on an escalator in a Tel-Aviv department store. Riding home in Queens, New York, a cab driver did a double take as he realized who I was. I don't usually recognize them because they were, after all, young boys on the day of liberation. I, on the other hand was an adult when they last saw me, and despite a few more pounds and a few lines, my face didn't change that much and it is still familiar to them. Today they are grandfathers, but they still remember and appreciate my efforts on their behalf.

Of the 3,200 that came in my transport, I knew of only eleven that were still alive at the end of the war. After liberation, I had become an old man, older than I am today in terms of strength and energy. I cared about nothing except going from day to day. The effects from all of the suffering I had gone through finally took their toll. I was very sick and it took a long time until I got better.

In the camp, I had been motivated by two goals—saving the children and helping other inmates, but now, with the camp liberated, the tremendous strain and stress of the long struggle to survive and help others finally caught up with me.

Shortly after the camp was liberated, the Americans discovered a tunnel in the quarry where the Germans had hidden millions of dollars worth of jewelry, gold, and other valuables taken from their victims. Handelsman and I watched from our window as they carted it off in trucks. We could have gotten rich just from the stuff that dropped off the trucks as they went by. But we didn't have the desire to take even a ring or a watch. It was as if we were dead. Whatever energy we had before, had disappeared.

When we first received regular food, we devoured it, despite the fact that we knew that it was dangerous to do so after being starved for so long. But you just couldn't help it. Our self-discipline disappeared. Self-discipline had been essential in Buchenwald. Those who possessed it had bettered their odds of surviving the camp. Those who didn't, were much more likely to die. But now that we were free, we could no longer contain ourselves.

You would think that now was the time to settle old scores, but it didn't happen all that much. Even though I'm a survivor myself, I'm not sure why we survivors didn't take revenge to a greater extent. Maybe it's because we were mentally and physically exhausted. The Russian soldiers, on the other hand, including the Jews among their ranks, took Germans, stripped them, tied them to trees and beat them senseless.

Much to my surprise, when I was liberated, I got everything back from the warehouse just as I had given it in, clothing, shoes, socks, and other personal items. I had assumed that I would never see these things again. They had even cleaned my suit. The dark green suit I wore during my first three months of incarceration, the suit that I sloshed through the mud in, had been immaculately cleaned and pressed. If I'd had money when I arrived in Buchenwald, they would have safeguarded it for me in the camp bank as well. This, however, was true only for those who came before 1940. After that, the possessions of new arrivals were permanently confiscated and given to German civilians.

As I ran my hands through the suit pockets, I felt what seemed like a piece of paper. I pulled it out and there, to my amazement, was a picture of my little daughter, Emma, who had been killed. It had been smuggled into my cell when I was first imprisoned in Radom and I had brought it with me to Buchenwald. The meticulousness of the Germans was once again demonstrated by what I found on the back of the photo. They had carefully written my name "Yankel Werber" and my prisoner number, 7197, on the back of it six years earlier, just in case it got separated from my other belongings. Even though we were like dirt to the Nazis and even though we were not expected to live, they still found it necessary to have everything properly labeled, recorded and stored.

Words cannot describe my feelings when I laid my eyes on this precious photograph. It had little significance for the Nazis, of course, but nothing could have been more meaningful to me. Knowing that Emma had been murdered made it extremely painful to look at, but I could not tear my eyes away. When I had first come to the camp with that picture, she had still been alive. As I looked around me and saw other inmates standing nearby, laughing and joking about what they were going to do now that they were liberated and who they were going to see, I was suddenly engulfed by a wave of emotion. I collapsed to the ground and began sobbing, looking at Emma's picture through tear-filled eyes. I had gone for years without crying, but now I could no longer hold back my feelings.

My mind had often drifted to thoughts of my family and, especially, my daughter, while I dragged impossibly heavy loads day and night as a "horse," or labored in other commandos. Thinking about how much I loved them, and how someday I might see them again had given me the strength to go on. At the same time, I had found it difficult, even impossible sometimes, to visualize what my daughter looked like physically. I had been through so much, she had been so small, and I did not have a chance to be with her for very long. And so now I was grateful that at least I had this one tangible reminder of her and that I could at least look at it and, in this small way preserve her memory.

Little by little I learned the details about individual family members. My sister Rivka's children, Fela and Moishele, and their father, were hidden in different monasteries in Belgium during the war. They survived the war, but soon afterwards Moishele was killed when a hand grenade he had picked up while playing outside exploded in his face. He was a wonderful child who was especially talented in art. A few of his charcoal sketches remain in our possession and are greatly treasured. Fela, whose last name is now Majzner, lives in Brooklyn and is married to another former Buchenwald inmate.

Another niece, Fela Werber Iliard, now lives in Israel. She's a daughter of my brother, Daniel and his wife, Nycha. Fela and her brother Zyniek were the only two members of my family who remained in Radom after the massive deportation of Jews in 1942. Realizing how desperate the situation was, they tried to escape from the ghetto.

Fortunately, our Polish friend, Jan Wojtas, came to their rescue. He gave Fela his daughter Felicia's birth certificate. In Warsaw she was able to use it to obtain a passport with her picture on it and she became Felicia Wojtas. With her blonde hair and long braids, she looked like a typical Polish girl and no one suspected otherwise.

As for Zyniek, his friend Jerzyk Weingarten had connections with a friend in Warsaw and was able to get false Christian papers for himself, another friend, Moniek Opatowski, and for Zyniek. According to plan, a Jewish member of the Underground named Adam, showed up in the ghetto masquerading as an SS officer, with an "order" to transfer Fela, Zyniek, Moniek, and Jerzyk to another ghetto or camp. They were taken outside to a waiting car and thus escaped the fate of so many other Jews. Fela, Zyniek, and their friends were placed in different locations throughout Warsaw, but Fela, afraid of being found out, volunteered to work in Germany as a "Polish maid."

But it was never safe to stay in one place too long. Fearing detection in Germany, Fela returned to Warsaw where the Underground helped her, Zyniek, and his friends escape from Poland. Their plan was to reach Palestine. They went first to Swiaty Mikulas, a town in Slovakia and from there to Hungary where they were helped by various Jewish organizations. When the Germans invaded Hungary on March 19, 1944, their situation became very dangerous and they fled to Rumania. Eventually they reached the port of Costanza and set sail for Palestine.

There were three boats, all of them filled to more than capacity, with Jewish refugees seeking to illegally enter Palestine despite the refusal of the British to allow Jews in. The Bulbul had about 450 passengers, the Marina 350, and the Mercury 300. Fela, with her group of Noar Zioni, was on the Bulbul. Zyniek and his friends were with the Hashomer Hatzair contingent on the Mercury. Then, the next day, there was an awful catastrophe. The Mercury exploded after suffering a direct hit from a German torpedo. It went down and all aboard were killed. After all their suffering, adventures and gallant efforts, this is how the struggle ended for Zyniek, Jerzyk, and Moniek. And Fela saw it happen right before her very eyes.

The Marina and the Bulbul continued on to Ankara, Turkey. Upon landing, the passengers were taken in wagons pulled by oxen to the railroad station. From there they went to Syria and then to Palestine, where they were taken to the infamous British prison in Atlit. Once there, they were helped by the Jewish Brigade. One of the officers, a Radomer named Menashe Blatman, recognized Fela and, after a one week quarantine period, brought her to her Uncle Izhak in Haifa.

Later, Fela joined Kibbutz Tel Itzhak. By chance, Shlomo Iliard, my comrade from the bricklayer's commando in Buchenwald, also managed to get into Palestine after liberation with the help of the *Brichah*, the illegal *aliyah* movement. By chance, he was sent by a contractor to a job on Fela's kibbutz in 1945. When he heard there was a Werber on the kibbutz, he was curious to know if she was a relative of mine. He found her, introduced himself and told her that he had worked together with me in Buchenwald. Since Fela had known that my ashes had been buried in Radom, she was skeptical about Shlomo's story. To make sure he was telling the truth she showed him a family picture and said: "Pick out my uncle." And, of course, he did. They became friends, fell in love, and got married.

Fela and Shlomo had two children. But life in Israel was hard and they accepted an invitation from relatives to move to Brazil. When they saw how much assimilation there was in that country, they returned to Israel with their children. Remaining Jewish was more important to them than getting rich. Shlomo became an administrator in the northern Galil town of Carmiel where he was one of the very first settlers. They still live there today. They suffered yet another great tragedy in their lives. Their son, Dani, was killed in an Israeli army training accident. It had been his dream to be a doctor and a soldier in the Israeli Army. They now remain with their daughter, Esther and two grandchildren. They never got over their son's death.

It took quite a while, but finally I felt well enough to travel and I went to Radom to look for Fela and Zyniek. At that time, I didn't know anything about their efforts to reach Palestine. When the Americans turned Buchenwald over to the Russians on July 3rd, I decided to remain in the camp, thinking that it would be easier to get to Radom from the Russian-occupied areas than from territories controlled by the Western powers.

Shortly thereafter I left Buchenwald with a group of other Jews who also wanted to look for their families in Poland. It was a long and terrible journey. The train was forced to stop about 25 miles away because the tracks had been bombed. We wound up traveling by foot and hitching rides with horse-drawn wagons and trucks. We were stopped many times by soldiers who demanded to see our papers before allowing us to continue. This delayed us considerably and what should have been an eight hour trip, took more than two weeks. We slept in abandoned German houses, eating whatever food had been left in them by their former occupants.

When I finally arrived in Radom, I met Yankele Weingarten. He told me the whole terrible story about how his son, Jerzyk and the others, including Zyniek, were killed on the Mercury after leaving Costanza. He also told me that Fela had made it to Palestine. When I heard this I felt there was no longer any reason to remain in Radom. Besides, people warned me to leave because several returning Jews had been killed there at night. The Poles were afraid that the Jews would now try to reclaim property they "abandoned" when they were taken to the camps.

Before I left I met a man by the name of Zukier, who was with me in Buchenwald: "I'm not a Jew anymore." he said:

"What happened?," I asked him. "You married someone not Jewish?"

"No, I married no one, but I've had enough with being Jewish." Today, he lives in Australia. The fact is that after the war, many people didn't want to be Jewish, but that feeling lasted only a short time for most of the survivors.

I decided to leave Radom that day. Walking around the city I felt like I was walking through a cemetery. I remembered the faces of the storekeepers and those who had lived behind each window. All the people I had known were gone, gone forever. I went to my father's house and knocked on the door, but the Pole who lived there refused to let me in. I managed to look in through the partly opened door and I saw that our furniture was still there, and in the same place. The man began screaming: "Get out of here before I kill you!" No doubt, he was thinking that I had come to reclaim my father's property. Then the wife of the building's superintendent recognized me but I told her she was mistaken. I left quickly and walked around the neighborhood, to my old school and the park where I used to play as a child. Looking at Radom for the last time, I knew that it could never be the same again. My heart felt like it was broken into many small pieces. I left that evening.

From there I traveled to Lodz, where it was somewhat safer for Jews. There was a registry of survivors in Lodz where Jews put their names on a list, hoping that their friends or relatives would find them. I saw my sister-in-law's name on it, Helen Alter. She lived near Lodz, in a suburb. Before the war she had been a chemist. I took a streetcar to see her and we had a very emotional reunion. She had assumed I was dead. My sister-in-law offered to get me an excellent job working in the government's Commerce Department. They were looking for educated people to work in the various government offices. I thanked her but told her:

"I'm not staying in Poland. But if you could help me get to Prague, where people are making arrangements to go to Palestine, I would really appreciate it." Within a few days she had prepared papers and had bought me a train ticket and a hat. She also gave me a letter stating that I was traveling for the purpose of buying rabbit skins which are used in the manufacture of felt hats for the Polish Government. Finally, she told me to put the ticket in my hatband when I sat on the train and to pretend that I'm sleeping. In this way, when the conductor checks, he'll just take the ticket, punch it, and won't ask me any questions. And this is exactly what happened.

When I arrived in Prague, I went to the offices of the Joint Distribution Committee. They sent me to a shelter where Jews from all over were staying. There I learned that you couldn't go to Palestine from Prague. Instead, it was necessary to go first to Germany and then to Italy. Coincidentally, I also met a Radomer who informed me that a cousin of mine, Itamar Werber, and other Radomer, were staying in Garmisch-Partenkirchen, Germany.

Most of these Radomer men had been liberated in Mittelwald, near Garmisch, after a forced march from Dachau. The Nazis had ordered them to lie down in a field to be shot. But a local German woman saw what was about to happen and convinced the guards not to kill them. In this way their lives were saved.

A few days later, I overheard some self-proclaimed *"machers"* confiding to some eager refugees who had paid them for assistance that a train was leaving for Germany the next day. To catch it they should be at the train station at a particular time. Others also overheard this and even though we had no money, we all went down to the station. A mob of people were waiting there, maybe 300 Jewish refugees. I just stood there as the names of those who had previously secured seats on the train were called out. "Moishe Goldberg! Chaim Friedman! Yaakov Gross!," and so on. Ten people would come out claiming to be Moishe Goldberg or Chaim Friedman. It was impossible to figure out who the real Moishe Goldberg or Chaim Friedman was, since no one had any documents. It was complete chaos. The Czech police were there and they were very polite. "Please wait in line," they begged. "Everything will be all right." And they continued to call out names until the train came. Suddenly everyone began running towards the train. They tried to climb in through the windows. Well, I saw the door was open and nobody was going through it. So I just walked right in and found a seat, and traveled to Garmisch-Partenkirchen in unaccustomed style.

I had a joyful reunion with my cousin, Itamar. We cried for hours, both from happiness and sadness, as we told each other what we went through during those awful years. At this time I learned why I had almost been released at the beginning of my stay in Buchenwald. My family, through the *Judenrat*, had bribed the SS with a large sum of money in an effort to obtain my freedom. After waiting about a month, they were shocked to receive a notice from the Judenrat stating that I had died in Buchenwald and that for a hefty fee, they could now purchase my ashes for burial.

Now that the war was over, the German population felt truly defeated. The German soldier without his uniform, no longer felt all-powerful. We could have moved into any place we wanted. All we had to do was register at City Hall.

But the truth was that we survivors wanted to stay close together even if it meant twenty people living in a single apartment. This was what we needed emotionally—to feel that we belonged somewhere. I moved into Itamar's apartment which already housed fifteen other men from Radom, most of whom I knew. We were once called scum. We were now called displaced persons. We D.P.s were struggling to rebuild our lives. We wanted desperately to recreate the sense of community and family that we had before the war. We searched for each other, for husbands and wives, brothers, sisters, and boyfriends and girlfriends. Everybody wanted to feel connected again to the world that once was.

The living conditions in this place were not so great but we shared everything, food and household duties, just like a family. We had ration cards but this was insufficient for our needs and everyone pitched in to help obtain more food. Srulek Rosenzweig worked in the American Army kitchen and brought us leftovers. The rest of us sold cigarettes, whiskey, household items, etc. It was so crowded that, for a while, I slept on a table that I shared with another fellow, using a window curtain as a blanket. His name was Moishe Rontal and he had been the new *chazzan* in Radom; he later became a cantor in Chicago.

When some women acquaintances from Radom came to Garmisch, we felt like our sisters had arrived. I found them apartments, clothing, and food, and shared everything with them. I took them to dressmakers and beauty parlors. They needed to feel like human beings that others cared about and we understood that very well. And it worked. Little by little life began to acquire real meaning again for them.

It was here that I met Millie, who was to change my life. Actually, she was a distant relative. Her parents were wonderful people. She was beautiful and had a truly fine character; a really nice person, who was quiet but who knew her own mind as well. In a way, she was almost like a child to me since she was considerably younger than I. Twelve years separated us. I was 30 years old then and she was eighteen. Due to this age difference, I didn't know her in Radom for when I was eighteen in Radom, she was only six years old.

I fell in love with Millie the day I met her, but I lacked the courage to tell her of my true feelings. I worried that I was too old for her. In the meantime, other suitors approached her, but, fortunately for me, she did not respond to them. I could not stop thinking about Millie. She became the center of my life. I lay awake nights debating with myself as to what I should do. Was I really too old? Should I declare my love for her and propose marriage? I was forced to make a decision when I learned that a man ten years older than I had expressed his interest in her. That being the case, I saw no reason why I shouldn't make my intentions known too.

One day, not long after this, we were sitting in a corner of the apartment, talking about our wartime experiences. Suddenly, overcome by emotion, I took Millie into my arms, held her close, and said softly:

"I love you very much and if you don't mind the fact that I'm older than you I'd like to marry you." Her response was:

"I've been waiting for this moment since the day I met you."

Upon hearing this, I was overjoyed. To this day, I cannot describe the feelings of both happiness and relief when I realized that my dream would come true.

Millie's father and her Uncle Yisrael had heard after the war that she and her aunt were no longer alive, that they had gone to their deaths in the crematorium at Auschwitz. So they decided to emigrate illegally to Palestine via Italy and begin a new life there. In the meantime, Aunt Gitele, Yisrael's wife, arrived in Garmisch with her young niece, Millie. She was looking for her husband, and Millie was trying to find her father. When Gitele heard that her husband and Millie's father had left for Italy she went to Milan to look for them.

Millie remained in Garmisch with our cousins, Zosia and Regina, and waited for Gitele to return. In the evening, we all got together and exchanged stories about our experiences during the war. Millie was twelve years old when the Germans entered Radom. By the time she turned fourteen she was working under inhuman conditions in a munitions factory. Her mother, at age forty-one, was considered too old to work in the factory and in 1942, she was deported to Treblinka where she perished in the gas chambers. Millie's father stayed in Radom and was working in a different factory, with no opportunity to see or help Millie. Thus, she was completely cut off from her parents. Not an aggressive type of person, she relied heavily on her Aunt Gitele to assist her.

Eventually, Millie was sent to Auschwitz where she went through a living hell. From there she was transferred with Aunt Gitele to a munitions factory in Lippstadt. As the war drew to a close, Millie, along with other Jewish women, went on a "death march" and ended up in Kaunitz, where they were liberated.

What was remarkable about Millie was that even though she had suffered tremendously as a child, these experiences did not embitter her. While, of course, saddened by everything that had happened, she was still able to give of herself to and to show great love and kindness to others. And people, in turn, adored and respected her.

When Gitele arrived in Milan, she learned that Yisrael and Millie's father had gone to Bari, which was a departure point for Palestine. Millie and I hadn't heard from Gitele for quite some time, and we became concerned. Communications were difficult. We couldn't telephone or write to find out what was going on. So we decided to follow Gitele to Milan. We took a train filled with Italian POWs from Russia. When we reached Milan, we learned that Millie's aunt had found her husband and Millie's father and had returned with them to Germany to look for us. In other words, we came to Italy to look for them just as they were leaving Italy to look for us in Germany! So naturally, we turned around and tried to go back to Germany through Austria but this turned out to be quite an adventure.

We decided to cross over into Germany, via Austria, by going through the Italian Alps. This was a crazy idea because it was winter and we had no mountain-climbing experience, but we never considered the dangers involved. We had never seen a mountain in Radom, and certainly nothing as big as the Alps. And here we were, trying to cross them to Austria, in the winter, when they were full of snow! Those were just crazy times. We still didn't have any possessions, just the clothes on our backs.

To tell the truth, we began our journey on a train bound for Germany. But when they checked our papers, they found that they were not in order and we were removed from the train and thrown into jail. It wasn't like the trip to Italy when the train was over-crowded with people and they weren't able to examine everyone's papers too closely.

Well, we couldn't speak the language and we were terrified. After they had pushed us into a jail cell where it was pitch black, we remained standing for maybe half an hour, afraid even to move. We knew there were two people there but we could only make out the whites of their eyes and so we said nothing. Gradually, how-ever, we began to get used to the darkness. Suddenly we heard a scream: "Manya! Jakub!" It turned out that our good friends from Radom, Manya and Alter Singer, were in the same cell and had recognized us. You can't imagine what it was like. It was as if we had seen *Moshiach*. Relieved and delighted, we hugged and kissed each other.

After a few days the four of us were transferred to a camp for refugees, Jewish and non-Jewish, from all over. It was not a well guarded place and we decided to escape with the other couple by jumping over a fence. We were not given any food, we didn't know what would happen to us there, and we still wanted to re-turn to Germany. We got on a freight train and met a band of smugglers and told them how we were arrested. After asking us if we could walk well, they offered to help us cross the Italian-Austrian border. At a certain point, the smugglers began jump-ing off the train, and urged us to join them. Our friends listened to them, but we didn't because we thought the train was going too fast. Luckily, the train slowed down a little further on and we jumped from the train.

We began making our way back to where we thought the smug-glers were. To do so we had to cross a swift running river. It was December, the water was ice cold, and it was getting dark. I don't know how we were able to make it across, but we did. Shortly after that we caught up to the smugglers and rejoined their group.

Unfortunately, I banged my knee against a tree stump as we began climbing the mountains and it slowed us down. So the smug-glers abandoned us because we couldn't keep up with them.

Now we were on our own and it was here that we got into real trouble. We climbed up the mountain, and when we reached the top, we stopped to rest in an old shed used for animals. It was cold and lonely and we were frightened. As we sat there shivering, we heard noises coming from animals that were moving about in the darkness. Looking around, we saw nothing but a white cover of snow on the slopes. The problem was we didn't know where it was deep and where not and we were afraid that we might sink into a snowdrift and that would be the end of us.

Suddenly I noticed a small light far below us. As I looked down, I could make out the outlines of what looked like a cottage. Realizing that if we stayed where we were we would freeze to death, we decided to take a chance and slide down. The problem was that within seconds we picked up speed and started going so fast that I was sure we were going to be killed. As a last resort, Millie hooked her foot around a tree to stop us and by some miracle we were able to come to a halt without breaking our necks.

We saw a house and tried to reach it. We hadn't eaten for two days. When we got there we discovered that we were still in Italy. We asked the owner of the house, a simple peasant, for a piece of bread but he said he couldn't give us anything. We could see they were really poor. Their cow was in the middle of the room where they were sleeping. The man said: "I have a lot of children and I don't have enough food for them." Millie had a ring. She took it off her finger and gave it to the man, saying: "Here. Take this ring. Just give us a piece of bread." But it was no use. He said: "I can't do it." Disappointed and starving, we left and continued on our way, slipping and sliding down to the bottom of the mountain.

Now we found ourselves right on the border. We were so frozen by then that the threads from my underwear had actually penetrated my skin and I couldn't separate my clothing from my body. Everything had become frozen solid. And here we were in a small town walking on the street, covered with mud and ice, looking as if we came from another world which, in fact, was true. In a way it was almost funny because Millie had to walk directly behind me so people wouldn't see the pieces of flesh that were sticking out from my pants.

In an attempt to avoid attracting attention, we pushed ourselves into the middle of a group of Italian laborers who were crossing into Austria. This worked and that's how we made it over the border. We looked around to get our bearings and saw a tavern nearby. We went inside to warm up so that I would be able to pry the clothing from my flesh. Thank God, the restaurant let us in to warm up by the oven or we'd have died from the cold.

We came back to Germany and linked up with Millie's family in Garmisch-Partenkirchen. They knew already that I was alive but it was still very emotional to meet again. Of course, it was a reunion mixed with sadness because when we saw each other it sort of brought home to us that Millie's mother and brother were dead.

Millie and I were married on January 24, 1946. I'll never forget the day. Garmisch was covered by a clean blanket of white snow. The sky was a gorgeous shade of blue with not a cloud to be seen. We rode to City Hall in a horse-drawn sleigh with bells that rang and which were attached to the horses. The clerk, a German with a gentle voice and a smile on his face, delivered a short sermon which concluded with a blessing, and gave us our marriage license. As I looked at him I wondered: "Where was he and what was he doing a year ago? Could he have been a guard in a concentration camp?"

On the way back we held hands without saying a word, each of us lost in our thoughts. Our hearts were filled with happiness and with hope for a new life together. We arrived at our cousin's apartment for the wedding party. As we walked in, we saw Aunt Gitele and some of our friends, all survivors. Everyone was busy preparing food and setting up a big table for about twenty guests. Getting the food was no easy matter. It was necessary to travel to different towns to obtain it. After all, the war had just ended. The party itself was simple—no photographer, no music, and certainly no smorgasbord and Viennese table. But that didn't matter. What was important was that we were together and married.

As we stood there, listening to Uncle Yisrael perform the religious ceremony, all of us had tears of both happiness and sorrow in our eyes. Some people could not control themselves and sobbed quietly as they thought of all those close to them who had tragically not lived to see this joyous day. Following the ceremony, everyone sat down to eat and talk. We stayed late into the night, singing Yiddish and Polish songs, both sad and happy, that we remembered from our childhood about a world that was lost and which could never be the same again.

Afterwards we left Garmisch and went to the D.P. camp in Stuttgart, because that was where our friends were going and that's where the offices were located to process those who wanted to go to the United States. Eventually, we received an affidavit from my brother Mannes, who lived in Beacon, New York, and who had come to America before World War I. The problem was that the affidavit was only in my name and I refused to go without Millie, her father, and my nephew, Sidney, with whom I had been reunited shortly after the wedding. Sidney was the only surviving child of my sister, Chana Roiza. When we first met, we fell into each others' arms. I was astonished to see that he had survived. Seeing that I was so insistent, the Joint Distribution Committee found a way to get permission for all of us to go together.

We left in May, 1946 on a U.S. Army transport ship, the *Marine Perch*. Millie and I both became seasick on board and had to stay below on separate levels most of the time. But when she heard that we had almost arrived and that the Statue of Liberty could be seen in the distance, Millie dragged herself up the stairs. I was already on deck. But she had fainted, and as she came to, a man was helping her up, saying she needed air. And suddenly I recognized and hugged him. It was Kolpak! The very same man who had saved my life as I was near death, by carrying me on his shoulders to the hospital instead of to the crematorium.

As I stood on the deck, looking at the Manhattan shoreline, it suddenly came to me that I had been through enough adventures and suffering for several lifetimes—My prewar life in Radom, the war, imprisonment in Buchenwald, the loss of my whole family. On the other hand, I had gotten married and was now about to start life in a new country. I had no idea as to what lay ahead of me, but I knew one thing—that it was important to not only go forward with my life but to always remember where I had come from, the love that my parents had given me, and most of all, the values that they had instilled in me. This was their legacy and I was determined to pass it on to my own family.